W9-ADQ-648

WWE ULTIMATE
SUPERSTAR GUIDE

Written by Jake Black

CONTENTS

WWE **DON'T TRY THIS** AT **HOME, SCHOOL,** OR **ANYWHERE.**

"I'm a professional, with years of training and a lifetime of practice. And I still get hurt, sometimes badly. Don't try any of the moves you see in this book, yourself—at home, school, or anywhere—it can be very dangerous!"

AIDEN ENGLISH

IT TAKES A BRAVE MAN to step into the ring and sing songs about WWE opponents, but that's exactly what Aiden English does. Classically trained in musical theater, Aiden English calls himself "The Artiste," and he loves the spotlight. But don't let his artistry fool you. English is an incredible performer inside the ring, able to deliver moves that are just as powerful as his vocal chords.

Dramatic hand gestures used to express emotions in the ring

VAUDEVILLAIN

English was a member of a tag team known as The Vaudevillains. The Vaudevillains were a throwback to a time of circus performers and strongmen. The team competed against some of WWE's best tag teams.

SUPER STATS

HEIGHT: 6ft 3in (1.90m)

WEIGHT: 215lbs (97kg)

HOMETOWN: Chicago, Illinois

SIGNATURE MOVE: The Director's Cut—English hooks his arm under the arm of his opponent then, jumps in the air and slams him down to the mat.

MAIN RIVAL: Tye Dillinger

AJ STYLES

THE WWE UNIVERSE was shocked when this international sports entertainment star joined WWE by entering the 2016 Royal Rumble Match. Styles is confident to the point of arrogance, calling himself "The face that runs the place," and referring to *SmackDown Live* as "The house that AJ built." But Styles has proven his talents in the ring having captured the WWE Championship less than a year after his debut.

Styles' Initials and the birth dates of his children are tattooed on his side

BEATING CENA

Styles believed he had to defeat John Cena to prove he deserved his nickname "The Phenomenal One." Their rivalry played out in several matches, but Styles achieved his goal when he dethroned Cena as the top Superstar at *SummerSlam 2016*.

SUPER STATS

HEIGHT: 5ft 11in (1.80m)

WEIGHT: 218lbs (99kg)

HOMETOWN: Gainesville, Georgia

SIGNATURE MOVE: Phenomenal Forearm—Styles leaps from the top rope and connects his forearm with his opponent's face.

MAIN RIVALS: John Cena, Kevin Owens

AKIRA TOZAWA

REPRESENTING HIS HOMELAND of Japan in the inaugural WWE Cruiserweight Classic in 2016, Tozawa brought a unique style of action to WWE. He is known for his harsh kicks and hard-hitting suplex moves. Tozawa has used his skills to win matches all over the world. Now a staple of WWE's cruiserweight division on *RAW* and *205 Live*, Tozawa has his sights set on the Cruiserweight Championship.

Mouth guard protects teeth during hard-hitting matches

Compression sleeves help blood flow to muscles

UNWANTED MENTOR

The Brian Kendrick offered his services as Tozawa's mentor, but Tozawa wasn't interested in his guidance. Angered by this rejection, Kendrick attacked Tozawa at *205 Live* and a fierce match ensued. Tozawa emerged victorious.

SUPER STATS

HEIGHT: 5ft 7in (1.70m)

WEIGHT: 156lbs (71kg)

HOMETOWN: Kobe, Japan

SIGNATURE MOVE: Snap German Suplex—Tozawa grabs his opponent around their waist from behind and flips them backward over his head and into a pin.

MAIN RIVAL: The Brian Kendrick

ALBERT

ALBERT'S LEGENDARY CAREER in sports entertainment has spanned two decades. As a Superstar, he battled major opponents such as John Cena and Sheamus. He was also a member of several tag teams. Since retiring from in-ring competition in 2014, Albert has given his insight as a commentator on NXT and has trained new Superstars as the head coach at WWE's Performance Center in Orlando, Florida.

Three of more than 20 piercings

LEARNING FROM THE BEST

Albert uses his vast in-ring experience to guide future generations of WWE Superstars at the WWE Performance Center. He teaches them the moves and holds they'll need to succeed in WWE.

SUPER STATS

HEIGHT: 6ft 7in (2.01m)

WEIGHT: 331lbs (150kg)

HOMETOWN: Boston, Massachusetts

SIGNATURE MOVE: Cannonball —Albert seats his opponent in the corner of the ring and runs into a rolling somersault, smashing his massive frame into his victim.

MAIN RIVALS: Undertaker, John Cena

ALEXA BLISS

COMPETITIVE, DETERMINED, and vicious, "Little Miss Bliss" channels all her fury into ruling the WWE women's division. Her snide remarks and nastiness ringside have led to countless matches, which have resulted in championship victories. Bliss is the first Superstar to win both the RAW and SmackDown Women's Championships, and she doesn't intend to stop there.

Vibrant hair color is part of her signature style

BLISS-TERING BECKY

Alexa Bliss needed the 2016 SmackDown Women's Championship like she needed air to breathe. Only Becky Lynch stood in her way. Bliss faced Becky, defeating her in a Tables Match to win the Title.

SUPER STATS

HEIGHT: 5ft 1in (1.54m)

HOMETOWN: Columbus, Ohio

SIGNATURE MOVE: Twisted Bliss—Alexa climbs to the top rope, diving toward her opponent and rotating 180 degrees in midair before landing on top of them.

MAIN RIVALS: Becky Lynch, Bayley

ALICIA FOX

DID YOU KNOW?
Alicia Fox first appeared in WWE as Hall of Famer Edge's wedding planner!

NOT MANY SUPERSTARS can claim they've made history, but as the first African American woman to win the Diva's Championship, Alicia Fox can. Since that major achievement in 2010, Fox has continued to make a big impact. She constantly outfoxes the competition in the ring and takes down her foes with ease. Fox is now on the hunt for the Women's Championship. Those in her way had better beware.

Sneaky expression hints at dangerous intentions

SNEAKY MOVES

Fox's ambition doesn't just stretch to her own WWE career. She has been known to help her significant other, the Superstar Noam Dar, win matches by distracting his opponents or even protecting him from attacks.

SUPER STATS

HEIGHT: 5ft 9in (1.75m)

HOMETOWN: Ponte Vedra Beach, Florida

SIGNATURE MOVE: Scissors Kick—Fox hits her opponent in the midsection and leaps into the air, snapping her legs around their head and driving it to the mat.

MAIN RIVALS: Sasha Banks, Bayley

ALUNDRA BLAYZE

HAVING LEARNED ABOUT the world of sports entertainment in Japan, Alundra Blayze burst into WWE in the mid 1990s and revitalized the women's division. After winning the WWE Women's Championship and successfully defending it for two years, Blayze became the division's hottest star. Her accomplishments earned her legendary status and a spot in the WWE Hall of Fame.

Blayze is a master of many forms of martial arts, including kickboxing

MADUSA

Blayze left WWE for rival company WCW where she competed under the name Madusa. She dominated the WCW women's division, defeating opponents such as Rhonda Singh.

SUPER STATS

HEIGHT: 5ft 10in (1.77m)

HOMETOWN: Tampa, Florida

SIGNATURE MOVE: Bridging German Suplex—Blayze grabs her victim around their waist from behind, lifts them over her head, and slams them onto the mat.

MAIN RIVALS: Wendy Richter, Bull Nakano

ANDRADE "CIEN" ALMAS

ALMAS BROUGHT THE expertise he displayed as a sports entertainment star in Mexico to NXT in 2015. As a WWE Superstar, he pounds his opponents with fast-paced aerial moves and can boast victories over fearsome contenders such as No Way Jose and Tye Dillinger. NXT challengers need to watch out for this rising star.

DID YOU KNOW?

In Mexico, sports entertainment is called "lucha libre." Opponents compete in a six-sided ring and use high-flying moves.

One of many fedoras that add to Almas's distinctive style

LUCHADOR

Almas is known for using missile dropkicks to surprise his opponents. He leaps through the air just like a luchador—the name used for wrestlers in Mexico.

SUPER STATS

HEIGHT: 5ft 9in (1.75m)

WEIGHT: 210lbs (95kg)

HOMETOWN: Gómez Palacio, Durango, Mexico

SIGNATURE MOVE: Hammerlock DDT—Almas wrenches his opponent's arm behind their back before putting them in a facelock and driving them headfirst into the mat.

MAIN RIVALS: Tye Dillinger, Cedric Alexander

ANDRÉ THE GIANT

DUBBED THE EIGHTH WONDER of the world, no other Superstar in WWE history has had larger stature, literally or figuratively, than André the Giant. André was undefeated in in-ring competition for 15 years. He captured several championships, including the WWE Championship, and was known the world over. He is loved by Superstars and the WWE Universe. André's legend will live on forever.

Extraordinarily large head used to level opponents

HALL OF FAMER

Since 1993, the WWE Hall of Fame has commemorated the legendary Superstars who have made an impact on sports entertainment. It's not surprising that André, the biggest legend of all, was the first inductee into the Hall of Fame.

SUPER STATS

HEIGHT: 7ft 4in (2.25m)

WEIGHT: 520lbs (235.90kg)

HOMETOWN: Grenoble, France

SIGNATURE MOVE: Sitdown Splash —with his opponent lying on the mat, André slams his massive frame down on their chest.

MAIN RIVALS: Big John Studd, Hulk Hogan

APOLLO CREWS

IN GREEK MYTHOLOGY, the God Apollo was known to bring devastation to the ancient Greeks. His WWE Superstar namesake certainly aims to devastate his opponents with his powerful acrobatic moves. Crews is known as one of the physically strongest Superstars in WWE, but somehow he manages to perform with the agility of a cruiserweight.

Large biceps show Apollo's great strength

RAW AFTER 'MANIA

Rookie Superstar Apollo Crews defied expectations in 2016 when he defeated Tyler Breeze on *RAW*. Crews displayed incredible strength during the fierce battle—his debut match in WWE!

SUPER STATS

HEIGHT: 6ft 1in (1.85m)

WEIGHT: 240lbs (109kg)

HOMETOWN: Stone Mountain, Georgia

SIGNATURE MOVE: Standing Moonsault—while his opponent is lying on the mat, Crews backflips and lands on them chest down.

MAIN RIVALS: Heath Slater, Dolph Ziggler

ARIYA DAIVARI

ARIYA DAIVARI CAME TO WWE in 2016 representing Iran in the Cruiserweight Classic tournament. Displaying unmatched aggression in the ring, Daivari has built an intimidating reputation for himself as part of the Cruiserweight division on *RAW* and *205 Live*. Daivari takes his nickname, "The Persian Lion," to heart. Superstars had better watch out! This is one vicious predator.

Daivari's "keffiyeh," a traditional Middle Eastern headdress

THE LION AND THE GENTLEMAN

Daivari used his spectacular Frog Splash maneuver to teach a lesson in aggression to his *205 Live* rival Superstar, Gentleman Jack Gallagher.

SUPER STATS

HEIGHT: 5ft 10in (1.77m)

WEIGHT: 190lbs (86kg)

HOMETOWN: Minneapolis, Minnesota

SIGNATURE MOVE: Frog Splash —Daivari launches himself from the ropes and comes down with incredible force onto his prostrate opponent.

MAIN RIVAL: Jack Gallagher

ASCENSION

DID YOU KNOW?

Ascension fought in a huge 16-Man tag team match in 2016, teaming up with The Headbangers, The Vaudevillains, and The Spirit Squad.

"MYSTERIOUS" AND "DANGEROUS" are two words that describe this frightening tag team. Its two members, Konnor and Viktor, hail from a desolate place named The Wasteland. With seemingly supernatural abilities, they have laid waste to the tag team division, devastating their opponents in the ring and striking fear into the hearts of the WWE Universe.

Traditional Wasteland war paint

ASCENDING TO THE TOP

In 2013, Ascension began their record 344-day-long reign as NXT Tag Team Champions with a blistering win over Adrian Neville and Corey Graves.

SUPER STATS

NAMES: Konnor and Viktor

COMBINED WEIGHT: 487lbs (221kg)

HOMETOWN: The Wasteland

SIGNATURE MOVE: Fall of Man —Viktor rams into an opponent while Konnor sweeps their legs from under them.

MAIN RIVALS: American Alpha, The Hype Bros

15

ASUKA

DID YOU KNOW?
In 2017, Asuka surpassed Goldberg's 173-0 winning streak with 177-0 wins.

NO OTHER FEMALE SUPERSTAR has been as dominant as Asuka. She has won every match since her NXT debut in 2015. She then defeated Bayley to win the NXT Women's Championship in 2016 and held the title longer than any champion in NXT history. With her signature menacing smile, Asuka warns her opponents that she is tough to beat—she may be right!

Face paint worthy of a true warrior

MASKS OF A WARRIOR

Asuka wears traditional Japanese "Noh" masks to the ring. She wears these colorful but haunting masks to frighten and intimidate her opponents.

SUPER STATS

HEIGHT: 5ft 3in (1.60m)

HOMETOWN: Osaka, Japan

SIGNATURE MOVE: Asuka Lock—lying behind her opponent, Asuka forces them to submit by locking her arms around their neck and wrapping her legs around their waist.

MAIN RIVALS: Bayley, Ember Moon

AUTHORS OF PAIN

Authors of Pain's manager, Paul Ellering

THIS PAIR OF MONSTERS barrelled into NXT in 2016 declaring their intentions to take over the NXT tag team division. And take over they did! First they won the Dusty Rhodes Tag Team Classic tournament and then they claimed the NXT Tag Team Championship from #DIY. This powerful pairing is the definition of dominance.

Tough combat gear suggests the duo are ready for battle

THE DUSTY RHODES CUP

The prestigious Dusty Rhodes Cup is awarded to the winners of the annual Dusty Rhodes Tag Team Classic tournament. The Authors of Pain conquered 15 other teams to win the Cup.

SUPER STATS

NAMES: Akam, Rezar

COMBINED WEIGHT: 620lbs (280kg)

SIGNATURE MOVE: The Last Chapter—one team member puts their opponent in a facelock while the other rebounds from the ropes and delivers a flying punch.

MAIN RIVALS: American Alpha, #DIY

17

BAM BAM BIGELOW

ROUGHLY THE SIZE of an airplane, Bam Bam Bigelow was a powerful giant who could move like a cruiserweight. Living up to his nickname, "The Beast From The East," Bigelow used his combination of size and agility to win championships against legendary Superstars such as Goldberg and Tatanka. Bigelow joined forces with Diamond Dallas Page in May 1999 and the pair won the WCW Tag Team Championship twice.

Flames warn opponents Bam Bam has a hot temper

Tooth lost in a match with André the Giant

GAME TIME

Bigelow faced football icon Lawrence Taylor at *WrestleMania XI*. The eyes of the entire sports world looked on as the two titans collided in the ring. Taylor won the match, but Bigelow proved he had the skills to be a top attraction in WWE.

SUPER STATS

HEIGHT: 6ft 4in (1.93m)

WEIGHT: 390lbs (176.90kg)

HOMETOWN: Asbury Park, New Jersey

SIGNATURE MOVE: Greetings From Asbury Park—Bigelow drags an opponent onto the ropes and slams them headfirst down onto the mat.

MAIN RIVALS: Goldberg, Tatanka

BARON CORBIN

DID YOU KNOW?

Corbin entered the Dusty Rhodes Tag Team Classic tournament in 2015 with Rhyno. They made it to the finals but lost to Samoa Joe and Finn Bálor.

THIS FORMER PROFESSIONAL football player was dropped from the league for being too aggressive. Soon after, Corbin became WWE's "Lone Wolf," bringing his aggressive nature with him to the ring. Corbin now claws through the WWE roster with a canine ferocity and he shows no remorse in attacking his victims. He will stop at nothing until he has his hands on the WWE Championship.

Sneer betrays his disgust with everyone

TROPHY WIN

Baron Corbin was the last man standing at the end of *WrestleMania 32*'s André the Giant Memorial Battle Royal, winning the match's prestigious trophy.

SUPER STATS

HEIGHT: 6ft 8in (2.03m)

WEIGHT: 275lbs (124.73kg)

HOMETOWN: Kansas City, Kansas

SIGNATURE MOVE: End of Days —Corbin lifts his opponent up by one arm and swings backward, dropping them face-first onto the mat.

MAIN RIVALS: Dolph Ziggler, Sami Zayn

BATISTA

AS STRONG AS AN OX and as vicious as a wolf, it's no wonder Batista is called "The Animal." His in-ring style is hard-hitting and unpredictable. Armed with his powerful Batista Bomb move, he has captured no less than six World Championships. Accomplished Superstars such as Triple H, John Cena, and Undertaker have all been overcome by his tremendous skill.

Philippine flag honors Batista's heritage

THE GREAT EVOLUTION

Batista was a member of Evolution. The powerful faction was made up of four of the greatest Superstars of the past, present, and future: Ric Flair, Triple H, Batista, and Randy Orton.

SUPER STATS

HEIGHT: 6ft 6in (1.98m)

WEIGHT: 290lbs (131.54kg)

HOMETOWN: Washington D.C.

SIGNATURE MOVE: Batista Bomb—Batista locks his opponent's head between his legs, spins them up onto his shoulders, and slams them down onto the mat.

MAIN RIVALS: John Cena, Triple H

BAYLEY

DID YOU KNOW?
Members of the WWE Universe who support Bayley carry signs that read "Hugger Section" to WWE events.

AS A LITTLE GIRL, Bayley attended WWE events and dreamed of winning the Women's Championship. She grew up to live her dream, even going as far as defending and retaining the Women's Championship at *WrestleMania 33*. Having won the hearts of the WWE Universe, Bayley likes nothing more than giving an encouraging hug to girls who share her dream of one day becoming a WWE Superstar.

Thumbs up—one of Bayley's signs of encouragement

BATTLING BANKS

Bayley's fiercest rival is Sasha Banks. Their highly competitive matches earned the dueling Superstars the honor of contesting the first-ever Women's Iron Man Match in NXT.

SUPER STATS

HEIGHT: 5ft 6in (1.68m)

HOMETOWN: San Jose, California

SIGNATURE MOVE: Bayley-to-Belly Suplex—clutching her opponent around the chest, Bayley leaps and forces them down onto the mat.

MAIN RIVALS: Sasha Banks, Alexa Bliss

BECKY LYNCH

Steampunk style goggles

DID YOU KNOW?
Becky Lynch joined WWE as part of WWE's Women's Revolution. She joined forces with Charlotte Flair and Paige to form Team PCB.

THIS FIERY SUPERSTAR silences any doubters every time she steps into the ring. Lynch, the "Irish Lass Kicker," was the first female Superstar drafted to *SmackDown Live* in 2016, and went on to defeat greats such as Charlotte Flair and Alexa Bliss. Lynch loves sharing her witty humor with the WWE Universe. But when it comes to the ring, she is focused and deadly serious.

WOMEN'S CHAMPION

Lynch defeated five other Superstars in a Six Pack Challenge Match where six female Superstars competed to be the first to score a pin or submission at WWE *Backlash 2016*. Lynch went on to become the first SmackDown Women's Champion.

SUPER STATS

HEIGHT: 5ft 6in (1.68m)

HOMETOWN: Dublin, Ireland

SIGNATURE MOVE: Dis-Arm-Her —Lynch grabs her opponent's arm and pulls back on it.

MAIN RIVALS: Charlotte Flair, Alexa Bliss

THE BERZERKER

SEEKING TO CONQUER WWE and destroy any Superstars who dared to oppose him, this Viking warrior wreaked havoc in the ring. The Berzerker carried a sword and shield and called out his battle cry of "Huss! Huss!" to intimidate his opponents before matches. Between the ropes he used his exceptional height and strength to punish his adversaries with powerful kicks and big slams.

Viking-style helmet

Weapons used to intimidate rather than wound opponents

BATTLE ROYAL

The high point of the Berzerker's WWE career came on the July 6, 1992 edition of "Prime Time Wrestling" (the Monday night precursor to *RAW*) where he won a 40-Superstar Battle Royal.

SUPER STATS

HEIGHT: 6ft 8in (2.03m)

WEIGHT: 323lbs (146.51kg)

HOMETOWN: Parts Unknown

SIGNATURE MOVE: Big Boot —The Berzerker strikes with a big kick to his opponent's chest.

MAIN RIVALS: Undertaker, British Bulldog

23

BIG BOSS MAN

Nightstick used to discipline unruly Superstars

Prison regulation haircut

A FORMER PRISON guard with a nasty attitude, the Big Boss Man carried out his own brand of justice in WWE and always made sure his opponents served hard time in the ring. Boss Man became Mr. McMahon's private security officer when the WWE CEO needed protection from the wrath of an enemy, Stone Cold Steve Austin.

LAW ENFORCEMENT

The Big Boss Man serves his personal form of hard justice on his opponent, the Brooklyn Brawler, with his punishing Avalanche maneuver.

SUPER STATS

HEIGHT: 6ft 7in (2.01m)

WEIGHT: 330lbs (149.68kg)

HOMETOWN: Cobb County, Georgia

SIGNATURE MOVE: Boss Man Slam—Big Boss Man scoops his opponents up by their shoulders and slams them to the mat.

MAIN RIVALS: "Ravishing" Rick Rude, Big Show

BIG CASS

HE'S SEVEN FEET tall, and you can't teach that! But you can use it to your advantage in WWE. Since joining WWE in 2013, first in NXT and then on *RAW*, Cass has used his mammoth size to dominate his opponents in matches. Splitting from his longtime tag team partner, Enzo Amore, Cass has proven to be a giant among giants.

Fist taped to protect fingers

"S-A-W-F-T!"

Big Cass is a man of few words, but one of them is SAWFT (soft). He uses it to describe his opponents, spelling it out for them for better understanding.

SUPER STATS

HEIGHT: 7ft (2.13m)

WEIGHT: 276lbs (125.19kg)

HOMETOWN: Queens, New York

SIGNATURE MOVE: East River Crossing—Big Cass lifts his opponents across his chest and swings them behind him, slamming them down.

MAIN RIVALS: Gallows and Anderson, The Usos

BIG JOHN STUDD

NOT MANY SUPERSTARS could look André the Giant in the eye, but Big John Studd was one of them. Studd's colossal frame made him part of an elite group of WWE giants. To prove himself as a Superstar, he set his sights on defeating André. Their ongoing rivalry defined Studd's career, and while he could not defeat André, he did earn his respect and that of the WWE Universe.

Thick, heavy beard like a fairy-tale giant's

Massive robe could fit two average sized adults at the same time

ROYAL RUMBLER

Big men have advantages in over-the-top-rope elimination matches. This was no more evident than in 1989's Royal Rumble Match, which Big John Studd won, defeating 29 other Superstars.

SUPER STATS

HEIGHT: 6ft 10in (2.08m)

WEIGHT: 364lbs (165kg)

HOMETOWN: Los Angeles, California

SIGNATURE MOVE: Reverse Bear Hug—Studd grabs his opponents around the waist and holds them crushingly tight.

MAIN RIVAL: André the Giant

BIG SHOW

DID YOU KNOW?

Beyond WWE, Big Show also dominated the Slime Wrestling World Championship at the Nickelodeon Kids' Choice Awards in 2012!

FOR MORE THAN two decades Big Show has made his massive presence known by plowing through Superstars and winning multiple championships. Entertainment royalty such as The Rock, Undertaker, and Ric Flair has fallen at his hands. Billed as "The World's Largest Athlete" in WWE, he is certainly one of the most dominant.

Tiger tattoo on one shoulder—a lion is on the other!

Big Show's enormous chest is an estounding 64 inches (1.6 meters) all the way around

GIGANTIC CLASH

The WWE Universe learned how truly massive Big Show and Brock Lesnar were when Lesnar suplexed Big Show from the top rope and the ring collapsed beneath them on impact!

SUPER STATS

HEIGHT: 7ft (2.13m)

WEIGHT: 383lbs (174kg)

HOMETOWN: Tampa, Florida

SIGNATURE MOVE: Chokeslam —Show grabs his opponent by the throat by one hand, lifts them high in the air, and throws them down.

MAIN RIVALS: Undertaker, Kane

BILLIE KAY

THIS SUPERSTAR CALLS herself iconic and backs up the claim with aggression and skill in the ring. Kay grew up in Sydney, Australia, where she honed her competitive spirit playing basketball. Her cutthroat nature is the driving force behind everything she does. She's a vicious Superstar who is not afraid to go on the attack in matches, sometimes before her opponent is ready.

Ring gear in blue—Kay's favorite color

BATTLE BUDDIES

Billie Kay came to NXT in 2015 and was joined by her childhood friend and fellow Australian, Peyton Royce. They call themselves "The Iconic Duo," and do everything together, including helping each other win matches.

SUPER STATS

HEIGHT: 5ft 8in (1.72m)

HOMETOWN: Sydney, Australia

SIGNATURE MOVE: School Girl Crush—Kay lifts her leg and drives her boot into her opponent's face.

MAIN RIVALS: Asuka, Liv Morgan

BO DALLAS

ALL YOU HAVE to do is Bo-lieve —at least that's what Bo Dallas says! No one believes in Bo more than he does, and he wants everyone to have that same level of confidence. After all, his confidence was the driving force behind his NXT Championship win. Dallas's self assurance has grown even more since he joined "The Miz-tourage," The Miz's esteemed bodyguards.

Thumbs up means a vote of confidence

SOCIAL OUTCASTS

Dallas felt WWE wasn't giving him the respect he deserved. When he discovered other Superstars felt the same way, he created The Social Outcasts faction. The faction included Curtis Axel, Adam Rose, and Heath Slater.

SUPER STATS

HEIGHT: 6ft 1in (1.85m)

WEIGHT: 234lbs (106.14kg)

HOMETOWN: Brooksville, Florida

SIGNATURE MOVE: Running Bo-Dog—Dallas grabs his opponent high on their body, runs up the ropes, and drags them to the mat.

MAIN RIVALS: Curtis Axel, Neville

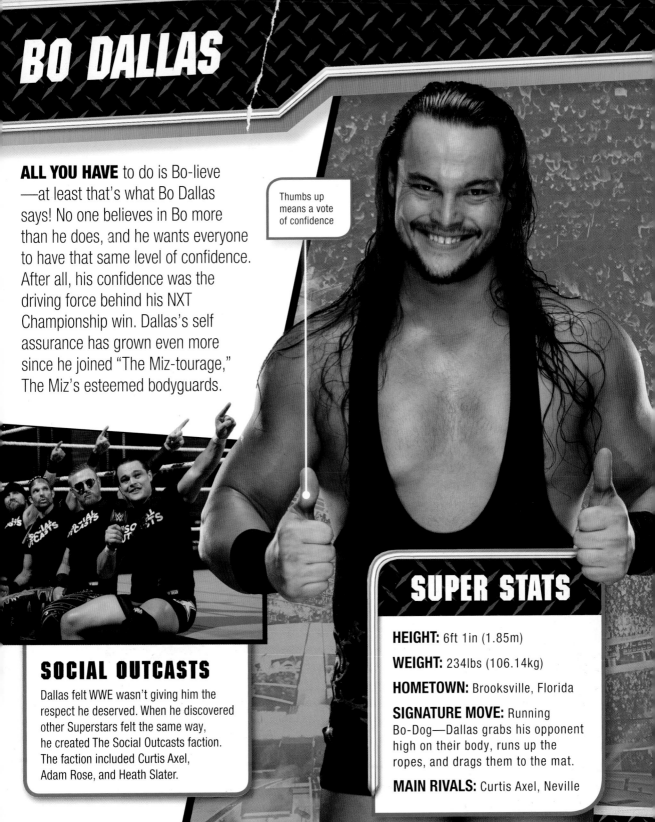

BOB BACKLUND

Backlund has had the same haircut for nearly 30 years!

HAVING EXPERIENCED LOSING streaks and other setbacks, Bob Backlund now works as a life coach and is certainly qualified to help Superstars such as Darren Young get their careers back on track. He knows what success feels like, having had a legendary in-ring career that spanned three decades. Backlund was inducted into the WWE Hall of Fame in 2013.

Towel for wiping away sweat mid-match

CHAMPION FOR ALL AGES

Bob Backlund proved his resilience when he won his second WWE Championship 16 years after winning his first by defeating Bret "Hit Man" Hart in 1994's *Survivor Series*.

SUPER STATS

HEIGHT: 6ft 1in (1.85m)

WEIGHT: 234lbs (106.14kg)

HOMETOWN: Princeton, Minnesota

SIGNATURE MOVE: Crossface Chicken Wing—Backlund twists his arms under his opponent's shoulders and in front of their face.

MAIN RIVALS: Bret "Hit Man" Hart, Iron Sheik

BOBBY ROODE

UPON ARRIVING IN NXT,
Bobby Roode vowed he would take WWE to new heights making it "glorious." He quickly made his mark by defeating Shinsuke Nakamura for the NXT Championship in 2017. As a proud champion, Roode arrogantly boasted that no opponent would ever be as glorious as he.

Robe sparkles like a disco ball when hit by bright lights

GLORIOUS ENTRANCE

Bobby Roode's entrance to the ring is spectacular. Countless white spotlights shine on him, causing his robe to sparkle. His theme song, titled *Glorious Domination*, is sung by a majestic choir.

SUPER STATS

HEIGHT: 6ft (1.82m)

WEIGHT: 235lbs (106.6kg)

HOMETOWN: Totonto, Canada

SIGNATURE MOVE: Glorious DDT—Roode holds his opponent's head under one arm and jumps backward slamming them to the mat.

MAIN RIVALS: Shinsuke Nakamura, Hideo Itami

THE BOOGEYMAN

EMERGING FROM THE WWE Universe's darkest nightmares came The Boogeyman. He haunted WWE for five years, competing with an unpredictable in-ring style. Whether it was his foaming at the mouth or eating live worms, The Boogeyman repulsed his opponents so much they couldn't focus on defeating him! He would appear and disappear in a flash and always with a terrifying warning: "I'm The Boogeyman, and I'm gonna get ya!"

Fur from unknown animal

Metal claws add to nightmarish appearance

FIT FOR A QUEEN

The Boogeyman had a favorite target for his gross tricks: Booker T's wife, Queen Sharmell. Sharmell found that The Boogeyman followed her everywhere she went and it terrified her— which is just what The Boogeyman wanted!

SUPER STATS

HEIGHT: 6ft 2in (1.87m)

WEIGHT: 260lbs (118kg)

HOMETOWN: The Bottomless Pit

SIGNATURE MOVE: Boogeyslam— The Boogeyman raises his opponent to his chest and slams them down to the mat, landing on top of them.

MAIN RIVALS: Booker T, Finlay

BOOKER T

DID YOU KNOW?
After winning the King of the Ring tournament, Booker suddenly discovered he had an English accent, which matched his newfound royalty status.

CELEBRATED AS

a five-time WCW Champion, Booker T is one the most decorated WWE Superstars of all time. He's won world championships, tag team championships, the King of the Ring tournament, and even served as *SmackDown* General Manager. Since retiring from the ring in 2011, Booker T has been a commentator for both *SmackDown* and *RAW*. He was inducted into the WWE Hall of Fame in 2013.

Sharp suit for work as a commentator or manager

WWE Hall of Fame ring given to inductees

HARLEM HEAT

Booker T and his brother Stevie Ray made up the tag team Harlem Heat. Together they won the WCW Tag Team Championship 10 times—more than any other tag team.

SUPER STATS

HEIGHT: 6ft 3in (1.90m)

WEIGHT: 256lbs (116kg)

HOMETOWN: Houston, Texas

SIGNATURE MOVE: Spinaroonie —in the style of breakdancing, Booker T spins on his back and neck, then leaps to his feet.

MAIN RIVALS: Triple H, Stone Cold Steve Austin

BRAUN STROWMAN

WITH A MIGHTY ROAR of his own name, Braun Strowman stalks his prey in the ring. Also known as "The Monster Among Men," Strowman began his career as a member of Bray Wyatt's stable, the Wyatt Family. But when Bray got drafted to *SmackDown Live*, Strowman remained on *RAW* and made a name for himself dominating Superstars such as Roman Reigns and Sami Zayn.

Incredible upper body strength helps Strowman punish opponents

REAL COMPETITION

To prove his power, Braun Strowman insisted that *RAW* General Manager Mick Foley give him some "real competition." Foley started putting Strowman in multi-opponent matches, allowing him to destroy two or three opponents at once!

SUPER STATS

HEIGHT: 6ft 8in (2.03m)

WEIGHT: 385lbs (175kg)

SIGNATURE MOVE: Reverse Chokeslam—Strowman grabs his opponent by the back of the neck, lifts them high in the air, and throws them down face first.

MAIN RIVALS: Roman Reigns, Brock Lesnar

BRAY WYATT

FROM DEEP IN THE WOODS, in a cabin lit only by a single candle, Bray Watt, "The Eater of Worlds," set out his plans to torment Superstars and instil fear in the hearts of the WWE Universe. Menacing Wyatt learns his opponents' greatest fears and forces them to face these terrors. Wyatt will take advantage of weakened courage and use it to defeat anyone in the ring.

Shirt reflects Wyatt's claim to instil fear in opponents

THE WYATT FAMILY

Bray Wyatt was the leader of a faction known as the Wyatt Family. The group of Superstars included Erick Rowan, Braun Strowman, and Luke Harper, who did Bray's bidding, attacked his foes, and helped him win matches.

SUPER STATS

HEIGHT: 6ft 3in (1.90m)

WEIGHT: 285lbs (129kg)

SIGNATURE MOVE: Sister Abigail—Bray leans his opponent's back over his knee, and twisting, whips the opponent over, slamming them onto the ground.

MAIN RIVALS: John Cena, Randy Orton

BREEZANGO

WHAT DO YOU GET when you cross a ballroom dancer like Fandango with a model like Tyler Breeze? The tag team Breezango! While matches are important to Breezango, they are also concerned with the Superstars' fashion choices. Known as The Fashion Police, the duo go undercover in the crowd at WWE events to investigate and call out any crimes of fashion.

Camera selfie stick for capturing fashion genius

NUMBER ONE CONTENDERS

Breezango shocked the WWE Universe when they won the Beat the Clock challenge in 2017 to become the number one contenders for the SmackDown Tag Team Championship.

SUPER STATS

NAMES: Fandango, Tyler Breeze

COMBINED WEIGHT: 456lbs (207kg)

SIGNATURE MOVE: Beauty in Motion—Breeze first kicks their opponent, then Fandango grabs them and flips them over his head.

MAIN RIVAL: The Usos

BRET "HIT MAN" HART

CALLING HIMSELF "the best there is, was, or ever will be" is a bold statement, but one that Hart has been able to back up. He used his superior technical skills in the ring to win countless matches and five WWE World Championships. An injury forced Hart to retire from competition in 2000. Since then, he has been *RAW* General Manager and he was honored with an induction into the WWE Hall of Fame in 2006.

Bret's skull-and-heart logo

HEALED HEART

Hart's greatest rival was "The Heartbreak Kid," Shawn Michaels. In 2010, after repeatedly clashing for several years, the Superstars set aside their differences and shook hands in a show of mutual respect, to the delight of the WWE Universe.

SUPER STATS

HEIGHT: 6ft (1.82m)

WEIGHT: 235lbs (106.60kg)

HOMETOWN: Calgary, Alberta, Canada

SIGNATURE MOVE: Sharpshooter —Hart wraps his opponent's legs around his own leg, turns his opponent onto their stomach and leans back.

MAIN RIVALS: Shawn Michaels, Stone Cold Steve Austin

THE BRIAN KENDRICK

HE FIRST DEBUTED

in WWE in 2003, amazing the WWE Universe with his aerial maneuvers and capturing the WWE Tag Team Championship on two occasions. The Brian Kendrick left WWE in 2009, but returned with a vengeance seven years later as part of the 2016 Cruiserweight Classic tournament. Now a seasoned veteran, Kendrick is determined to prove his superiority against less experienced cruiserweights.

DID YOU KNOW?
Prior to returning to the ring in 2016, The Brian Kendrick helped train NXT Superstars at the WWE's Performance Center.

Trademark jacket

Pirate flag carried in honor of one of Kendrick's heroes—the pirate Blackbeard

TRAINING BUDDIES

The Brian Kendrick was trained in sports entertainment by WWE Hall of Famer Shawn Michaels in his training school in San Antonio, Texas. One of Michaels' students was Daniel Bryan. Kendrick and Bryan were roommates during their training and remain close.

SUPER STATS

HEIGHT: 5ft 8in (1.72m)

WEIGHT: 157lbs (71.21kg)

HOMETOWN: Venice, California

SIGNATURE MOVE: Captain's Hook—Kendrick holds the top of his opponent's body and stretches it in a painful submission hold.

MAIN RIVALS: TJP, Akira Tozawa

BRIAN PILLMAN

UNPREDICTABLE is an understatement when describing the unhinged Superstar Brian Pillman. The professional football player turned WWE Superstar delighted in making his opponents, and the WWE Universe, try to guess what he would do next. This behavior gave Pillman the advantage in his matches —no opponent could fully prepare to face him!

Menacing grin strikes fear into opponents

THE HOLLYWOOD BLONDS

Early in his career, Pillman was one half of a tag team named The Hollywood Blonds. His blond, long-haired partner was "Stunning" Steve Austin, who, years later, would become "Stone Cold."

SUPER STATS

HEIGHT: 6ft (1.82m)

WEIGHT: 227lbs (103kg)

HOMETOWN: Cincinnati, Ohio

SIGNATURE MOVE: Air Pillman —Pillman would dive from the top rope, crashing down on top of his opponent.

MAIN RIVALS: Stone Cold Steve Austin, Goldust

BRIE BELLA

ALONG WITH HER twin sister, Nikki, Brie Bella joined WWE in 2008, shocking all by winning her very first match against the former Women's Champion, Victoria. In 2011, she shocked again by winning the WWE Divas Championship. Brie competed for the final time at *WrestleMania* 32 in 2016. Though retired, Brie has promised to return to the ring someday.

Headband helps differentiate Brie from her twin sister Nikki, who usually wears a cap

TWIN MAGIC

The Bella Twins look a lot alike, and have used that to their advantage in matches. When their opponent and the referee are distracted, the sisters sometimes switch places, allowing a ready and rested Bella to sneak a surprise victory!

SUPER STATS

HEIGHT: 5ft 6in (1.67m)

HOMETOWN: Scottsdale, Arizona

SIGNATURE MOVE: Bella Buster—Brie grabs her opponent by the back of the head, and leaping in the air drives them face down to the mat.

MAIN RIVALS: Natalya, Tamina

BRITISH BULLDOG

RUGGED AND PHYSICALLY powerful, British Bulldog would hold his opponents above his head to showcase his tremendous strength. He won several championships throughout his career. One of his most impressive victories was in Berlin, Germany in 1997 when he battled in an eight-Superstar tournament to become the first-ever WWE European Champion.

Ring gear with colors from the Union Jack, the national flag of the United Kingdom

FAMILY TUSSLE

Bulldog defeated his brother-in-law Bret "Hit Man" Hart to win the Intercontinental Championship in front of a huge crowd in the United Kingdom. At the end of the match, Bulldog's wife Diana celebrated by raising her husband's *and* brother's hands.

SUPER STATS

HEIGHT: 5ft 11in (1.80m)

WEIGHT: 260lbs (118kg)

HOMETOWN: Manchester, England

SIGNATURE MOVE: Running Powerslam—Bulldog lifts his opponent on his shoulder, runs, and throws them down.

MAIN RIVALS: Ken Shamrock, The Rock

BROCK LESNAR

BROCK LESNAR ENJOYS only one thing: hurting people. With a nickname to match his attitude, "The Beast" feels no remorse over the punishment he gives his opponents. Lesnar doesn't have friends—he doesn't want any. He only cares about winning matches and championships. His WWE achievements include being the only Superstar to have held the WWE and Universal Championships.

Mixed martial arts gloves

CONQUER THE STREAK

The WWE Universe were stunned at *WrestleMania 30* when Brock Lesnar defeated Undertaker in a brutal match, breaking his legendary 21-0 winning streak.

SUPER STATS

HEIGHT: 6ft 3in (1.90m)

WEIGHT: 286lbs (129.70kg)

HOMETOWN: Minneapolis, Minnesota

SIGNATURE MOVE: German Suplex—Lesnar grabs his opponent around the waist from behind and throws them backward over his head.

MAIN RIVALS: Undertaker, Roman Reigns

BRUNO SAMMARTINO

FROM EARLY CHILDHOOD, Bruno Sammartino was encouraged to be tough. During his two reigns as WWE Champion, Sammartino defeated countless opponents including WWE Hall of Famers "Superstar" Billy Graham and Gorilla Monsoon. Seen as a WWE icon by all in sports entertainment, Sammartino was honored with a place in the WWE Hall of Fame in 2013.

WWE Championship Title worn proudly

LONGEST REIGN

Sammartino won the WWE Championship from "Nature Boy" Buddy Rogers, and held it for nearly eight years—the longest title reign in WWE history!

SUPER STATS

HEIGHT: 5ft 10in (1.77m)

WEIGHT: 265lbs (120kg)

HOMETOWN: Pittsburgh, Pennsylvania

SIGNATURE MOVE: Bear Hug —Sammartino grabs his opponent in a hug around the waist and squeezes tighter and tighter.

MAIN RIVALS: "Rowdy" Roddy Piper, "Macho Man" Randy Savage

BRUTUS BEEFCAKE

Clippers, an exaggerated version of barber shears

NOBODY COULD "CUT AND STRUT" quite like Brutus Beefcake. He would stride around the ring slicing his hands in a scissorslike gesture—a warning of his habit of using clippers or scissors to cut the hair of his opponents against their will, which earned him the name "The Barber." Beefcake used his mastery of the Sleeper Hold to get victories—and hair clients! He was also known for his flamboyant outfits that looked like they'd been shredded by a lawn mower.

THE BARBERSHOP

Beefcake hosted a talk show segment on WWE TV called *The Barbershop*. The show was set in a mock salon and featured many memorable moments, including the breakup of popular tag team The Rockers.

BUDDY MURPHY

Strength gained through extreme sports such as rock climbing

FEARLESS TO A FAULT, Buddy Murphy has perfected some of the most spectacular high-risk aerial moves in NXT. But Murphy feels like he doesn't get the recognition he deserves from fellow WWE Superstars, and this has given him a nasty attitude. He is determined to get the respect he feels is due—by force if necessary!

TAG CHAMP

Murphy held the NXT Tag Team Championship for seven months with his then tag team partner, Wesley Blake. The pair used their combined strength in double attacks to defeat many opponents, including The Vaudevillains.

Red streaks demonstrate his hot temper

SUPER STATS

HEIGHT: 5ft 11in (1.80m)

WEIGHT: 227lbs (103kg)

HOMETOWN: Melbourne, Australia

SIGNATURE MOVE: Murphy's Law—Murphy hoists his opponent up, their legs in the air, and slams them down onto the mat.

MAIN RIVALS: Shinsuke Nakamura, Kota Ibushi

BUSHWHACKERS

DID YOU KNOW?

Bushwhacker Luke set a record for the shortest amount of time in a Royal Rumble Match. He lasted just four seconds.

POOR MANNERS

and a rough-and-tumble style may not have helped endear these cousins to high society, but they were beloved by the WWE Universe. The comical New Zealanders were known for their toothless smiles and arm-swinging strut. The tag team's goofy antics helped them stomp their way into the WWE Hall of Fame in 2015.

Bent arm ready for the "Bushwhacker Strut"

GREETINGS

The Bushwhackers showed affection for the WWE Universe by licking fans on their heads. This was made more memorable if the Bushwhackers had eaten their favorite meal beforehand: sardines!

SUPER STATS

NAMES: Butch, Luke

COMBINED WEIGHT: 496lbs (225kg)

HOMETOWN: New Zealand

SIGNATURE MOVE: Battering Ram —Bushwhacker Butch held his cousin Luke's head under his arm and rammed it into the stomach of an opponent.

MAIN RIVALS: Natural Disasters, Nasty Boys

CARMELLA

THIS BRAWLER calls herself "fabulous" and it's unwise to disagree. Carmella has a sassy attitude and the fashion sense to match. She deals out hard kicks and elbows and is skilled at escaping submission holds. Carmella currently has her eye on the SmackDown Women's Championship and she will turn on her friends—just like she turned on Nikki Bella and Naomi—to get it.

DID YOU KNOW?

Carmella won in the first ever Women's Money in the Bank Ladder Match in June 2017.

NXT TIES

While in NXT, Carmella joined forces with Superstars Enzo Amore and Big Cass. They liked to remind the NXT Universe that beauty like Carmella's is something you can't teach!

SUPER STATS

HEIGHT: 5ft 5in (1.65m)

HOMETOWN: Staten Island, New York

SIGNATURE MOVE: Code of Silence—Carmella wraps her legs around her opponent on the mat and stretches backward.

MAIN RIVALS: Becky Lynch, Nikki Bella

CEDRIC ALEXANDER

Alexander is never seen without his trademark necklace

AFTER AN IMPRESSIVE performance in the 2016 WWE Cruiserweight Classic tournament, Cedric Alexander joined WWE as a part of the cruiserweight division on *RAW* and *205 Live*. Alexander, who competed in sports entertainment around the world before coming to WWE, is known for his combination of hard-hitting kicks and high flying aerial maneuvers. There's nothing Alexander wants more than to be Cruiserweight Champion.

Taped hands allow for harder strikes

BATTLING DAR

For months, Cedric Alexander battled Noam Dar. Originally the two cruiserweights were competing for the affections of Alicia Fox, but their rivalry became personal. Alexander put an end to their rivalry by winning an "I Quit" match against Dar in 2017.

SUPER STATS

HEIGHT: 5ft 10ins (1.77m)

WEIGHT: 205lbs (92.99kg)

HOMETOWN: Charlotte, North Carolina

SIGNATURE MOVE: Lumbar Check —Alexander grabs his opponent from behind, throws them in the air and hits them with his knee.

MAIN RIVALS: Noam Dar, TJP

CESARO

Tuxedo is ripped off as Cesaro enters the ring

CESARO SPEAKS FIVE languages—and he's also an expert in the language of sports entertainment. This fine-tuned, athletic competitor displays incredible control and precision in his matches. He used these abilities in 2016 in a series of seven matches against the Superstar Sheamus. Although neither contender was the overall winner of the series, their respect for each other grew and they formed a tag team.

KING OF SWING

Cesaro got his nickname, "The King of Swing," because of his signature move. He has used this move to win matches against countless opponents on *RAW*, including Bo Dallas.

SUPER STATS

HEIGHT: 6ft 5in (1.95m)

WEIGHT: 232lbs (105kg)

HOMETOWN: Lucerne, Switzerland

SIGNATURE MOVE: Cesaro Swing —Cesaro holds his opponents by their legs, and spins in a dizzying circle.

MAIN RIVALS: Sheamus, The Hardy Boyz

CHAD GABLE

Headband keeps Gable's long hair out of his face during matches

HAVING COMPETED IN amateur wrestling at the 2012 Summer Olympic Games, Chad Gable knows the technical skills needed for in-ring competition. With his talent and experience behind him, Gable made a name for himself in NXT and then reigned over the tag team division with Jason Jordan. When Jordan left *SmackDown Live* for *RAW*, Gable refocused his efforts to try to win singles championships.

Ring gear is similar to gear worn in the Olympics

ALPHA MALES

Gable won the NXT and *SmackDown* Tag Team Championships as a member of American Alpha. In 2016, they became the first team to win the two titles in the same year.

SUPER STATS

HEIGHT: 5ft 8in (1.72m)

WEIGHT: 202lbs (91.62kg)

HOMETOWN: Minneapolis, Minnesota

SIGNATURE MOVE: Grand Amplitude—Gable flips his opponent backward over his head.

MAIN RIVALS: Kevin Owens, Rusev

CHARLOTTE FLAIR

KNOWN AS THE QUEEN of WWE, Charlotte Flair demands that everyone in the WWE Universe bow before her greatness. As the daughter of 16-time World Champion, Ric Flair, Charlotte is doing her upmost to build a legacy that's worthy of her family name. She has won the NXT Women's Championship, she was the final WWE Divas Champion before the title was retired in 2016, and she's a five-time RAW Women's Champion.

Sparkly clothing is reminiscent of her father's lavish robes

FAMILY FEUD

Charlotte idolized her father, Ric Flair, growing up. When she entered WWE, she was glad to have her dad by her side. But as Charlotte achieved more success, she felt she didn't need him anymore and publicly ended their relationship.

SUPER STATS

HEIGHT: 5ft 10in (1.77m)

HOMETOWN: The Queen City

SIGNATURE MOVE: Figure-Eight Leglock—Charlotte twists her opponent's legs with her own and leans back on her hands.

MAIN RIVALS: Becky Lynch, Sasha Banks

CHRIS JERICHO

UPON ENTERING WWE

in 1999, Chris Jericho declared he'd put the entertainment back into sports entertainment. The WWE Universe soon fell in love with his outrageous persona. Jericho is the first to tell people that he has been hugely successful in the ring. He was the first WWE Undisputed Champion and has been Intercontinental Champion a record nine times.

Jericho's scarves are "obscenely expensive"—he prides himself on it

Jacket sparkles and lights up during entrances

THE LIST OF JERICHO

Jericho keeps track of everyone who attacks him, offends him, or even annoys him in a book called "The List of Jericho." Those who have "made the list" better watch out—Jericho will get his revenge.

SUPER STATS

HEIGHT: 6ft (1.82m)

WEIGHT: 227lbs (103kg)

HOMETOWN: Winnipeg, Manitoba, Canada

SIGNATURE MOVE: Walls of Jericho—Jericho grabs his opponent's legs while on they are on their back, hooks them over his knees, turns them over, and leans back.

MAIN RIVALS: Kevin Owens, Dean Ambrose

THE COLONS

THESE CHARASMATIC COUSINS are always happy to share the beauty of their home island, Puerto Rico, by giving out pamphlets of the island to the WWE Universe and Superstars. In the ring, the Colons have made an impact on the WWE tag team divisions on *RAW* and *SmackDown Live*. The cousins won the WWE Tag Team Championship in 2012, and have since been on a quest to recapture the titles and prove their dominance and superiority.

White wrist strapping helps to distinguish Epico

Taino Sun symbol is of ancient Puerto Rican origin

OPPOSING ENZO

The Colons found their greatest success in recent years in matches against Enzo Amore and his then tag team partner, Big Cass. The Colons defeated Enzo and Cass in a match on *RAW* in 2016, using a double team attack on Enzo.

SUPER STATS

NAMES: Primo Colon, Epico Colon

COMBINED WEIGHT: 440lbs (199.58kg)

HOMETOWN: San Juan, Puerto Rico

SIGNATURE MOVE: Powerbomb Backbreaker—Epico lifts their opponent shoulder high and drops them onto the waiting knee of Primo.

MAIN RIVALS: American Alpha, Enzo and Cass

"COWBOY" BOB ORTON

ALSO KNOWN AS "ACE," "Cowboy" Bob Orton was the second of three generations of Ortons to enter WWE. He followed his father, Bob Orton Senior, and passed the legacy to his son, Randy Orton. During his time in WWE, "Cowboy" Bob Orton was known for his loyalty. He assisted his friend "Rowdy" Roddy Piper in a boxing match against celebrity contender Mr. T at *WrestleMania II* and tried to protect his son from Undertaker's wrath at *WrestleMania 21*. "Cowboy" Bob Orton was inducted into the WWE Hall of Fame in 2005.

Trusty hat—Orton was never without it

PERMANENT CAST

After breaking his arm in a match, "Cowboy" Bob Orton wore a cast. But while most broken bones heal within a few weeks or months, Orton's didn't. He wore the cast (and used it as a weapon in matches) for more than two years! Including his match against the Superstar Junkyard Dog.

SUPER STATS

HEIGHT: 6ft 1in (1.85m)

WEIGHT: 242lbs (110kg)

HOMETOWN: Kansas City, Kansas

SIGNATURE MOVE: Superplex —Orton hooks his opponent's head under one arm and lifts him up by the waist with the other arm, falling backward to the mat with a thud.

MAIN RIVALS: Don Muraco, Tito Santana

CURT HAWKINS

CURT HAWKINS LOVES to share "facts" about himself, such as "time waits for no man, except Curt Hawkins." He is the youngest WWE Tag Team Champion in history, winning the Title when he was just 22. Calling himself the "Prince of Queens," Hawkins believes he will take over *RAW* and become the WWE Universal Champion. He tells every Superstar in his way to just "face the facts."

Clenched fists ready to defend his "facts"

Short hair to make him look less like his former boss, Edge

THE EDGEHEADS

Hawkins and Zack Ryder were hired by the Superstar Edge to disguise themselves as Edge's lookalikes. The "Edgeheads" took poundings from Edge's opponents before the real Edge would join the match and defeat his wearied opponent.

SUPER STATS

HEIGHT: 6ft 1in (1.85m)

WEIGHT: 223lbs (101.15kg)

HOMETOWN: Queens, New York

SIGNATURE MOVE: Heat-Seeking Elbow—Hawkins dives off the top rope, landing with his elbow on the chest of his opponent.

MAIN RIVAL: Apollo Crews

CURTIS AXEL

AS THE GRANDSON of Larry "The Ax" Hennig and the son of "Mr. Perfect" Curt Hennig, this third-generation Superstar is on a mission to prove he's worthy of his family legacy. With tremendous technical skill, Curtis Axel defeated The Miz to win the Intercontinental Championship in 2013. Axel was also the final pick for *RAW* at the 2016 WWE Superstar Draft. Axel made the bold claim that the *RAW* General Managers had "saved the best for last." He believes it's his time to shine in the spotlight!

DID YOU KNOW?

Axel was originally known in WWE as Michael McGillicutty, but changed his name to pay tribute to his father and grandfather.

Axel's beard looks very similar to his grandfather's

HENNIG FAMILY

Axel's father, "Mr. Perfect" Curt Hennig, and his grandfather, Larry "The Ax" Hennig, were known for their close relationship. They did everything together, including training in the gym before matches.

SUPER STATS

HEIGHT: 6ft 3in (1.90m)

WEIGHT: 228lbs (103.42kg)

HOMETOWN: Champlin, Minnesota

SIGNATURE MOVE: Perfect-Plex —Axel bends his opponent and flips them over into a pin.

MAIN RIVALS: Bo Dallas, Enzo and Cass

DANA BROOKE

A BACKGROUND IN competitive bodybuilding means that Dana Brooke is not afraid to show off her toned muscles. She takes every opportunity to pose and flex to make her opponents nervous before a match. Brooke was aligned with fellow Superstar Charlotte Flair, but she has branched out on her own and is aggressively in pursuit of the *RAW* Women's Championship.

Sparkling ring gear is similar to that of Charlotte Flair

Exceptional strength gained from bodybuilding

PROTECTING FLAIR

Dana Brooke learnt a lot from her mentor, Charlotte Flair. Acting as Charlotte's bodyguard, Dana would often attack and berate Charlotte's opponents, including Sasha Banks, during matches.

SUPER STATS

HEIGHT: 5ft 3in (1.60m)

HOMETOWN: Cleveland, Ohio

SIGNATURE MOVE: Handstand Leg Hold—Brooke stands on her hands and wraps her legs around her opponent, dragging them to the mat.

MAIN RIVALS: Bayley, Emma

DANIEL BRYAN

SMALL IN PHYSICAL SIZE, but big on passion for sports entertainment, Daniel Bryan was always considered the underdog by WWE management and even his fellow Superstars. But to the WWE Universe, he is an inspirational hero. Propelled by his rallying "Yes!" chant, Bryan made it to the main event of *WrestleMania 30* where he won the WWE Championship. Bryan retired in 2016, and became the General Manager of *SmackDown Live*.

Bryan's beard has been affectionately referred to as "goat-like"

UNLIKELY PARTNERS

It would be difficult to find two Superstars whose personalities were less like each other's than Kane and Daniel Bryan. But when they formed a tag team called "Team Hell No," the pair proved that opposites can attract.

Simple ring gear for a business-minded Superstar

SUPER STATS

HEIGHT: 5ft 10in (1.77m)

WEIGHT: 210lbs (95kg)

HOMETOWN: Aberdeen, Washington

SIGNATURE MOVE: Yes Lock— Bryan wraps his arms under his opponent's shoulders and face.

MAIN RIVALS: Triple H, The Miz

DARREN YOUNG

IT'S POSSIBLE NO ONE works harder than Darren Young. He calls himself "Mr. No Days Off" because he never quits. Young is constantly trying to make himself better, whether that involves working out to increase his strength, training to improve his technique or focusing on his mental performance with his life coach, WWE Hall of Famer Bob Backlund. Young's dedication bought him the Tag Team Championship in 2015.

"#Block The Hate" is Young's anti-bullying slogan

NEXUS

Darren Young was one of seven rookie Superstars from NXT who felt disrespected by the *RAW* and *SmackDown* brands. The Superstars formed a faction called "The Nexus," and wrecked havoc on WWE as revenge.

SUPER STATS

HEIGHT: 6ft 1in (1.85m)

WEIGHT: 239lbs (108kg)

HOMETOWN: Miami, Florida

SIGNATURE MOVE: Crossface Chicken Wing—Young wraps his arms under his opponent's shoulders and applies pressure.

MAIN RIVAL: The Colons

DEAN AMBROSE

Wild-eyed expression reveals the chaos inside Ambrose's mind

PERSONAL HEALTH AND safety is not much of a concern to Dean Ambrose. Ambrose does what he has to in order to inflict pain on his opponents—even if it causes harm to himself. This reckless behavior has earned him the nickname "The Lunatic Fringe." His wild ways serve him well in the ring —Ambrose shocked his opponents and the WWE Universe with United States and WWE Championships wins in 2013 and 2016.

DID YOU KNOW?

Dean Ambrose holds the record for longest United States Championship reign at 351 days.

THE SHIELD

Ambrose was a member of a dominant faction named The Shield with Roman Reigns and Seth Rollins. The Shield, dressed in police S.W.A.T. gear, and plowed through several Superstars in NXT and WWE before separating in 2014.

SUPER STATS

HEIGHT: 6ft 4in (1.93m)

WEIGHT: 225lbs (102kg)

HOMETOWN: Cincinnati, Ohio

SIGNATURE MOVE: Dirty Deeds —Ambrose wraps his arms under his opponent's shoulders and slams them into the mat.

MAIN RIVALS: Chris Jericho, Seth Rollins

DEAN MALENKO

PREFERRING TO LET his actions in the ring speak for him, Dean Malenko is a man of few words. He is a focused athlete who uses classic maneuvers, which he executes perfectly. Malenko knows just about every move and countermove there is in sports entertainment and he always keeps his emotions in check, which makes him even more deadly!

Cool demeanor hides steely determination

THE MAN OF 1004 HOLDS

During his time in WCW, Malenko's greatest rival was Chris Jericho. Jericho annoyed Malenko by claiming to know four more holds than Malenko, a total of 1004. Malenko got the last laugh by besting Jericho in their matches.

SUPER STATS

HEIGHT: 5ft 10in (1.77m)

WEIGHT: 212lbs (96kg)

HOMETOWN: Tampa, Florida

SIGNATURE MOVE: Texas Cloverleaf—Malenko wraps his opponent's legs around his own and leans backward.

MAIN RIVALS: Chris Jericho, Eddie Guerrero

DIAMOND DALLAS PAGE

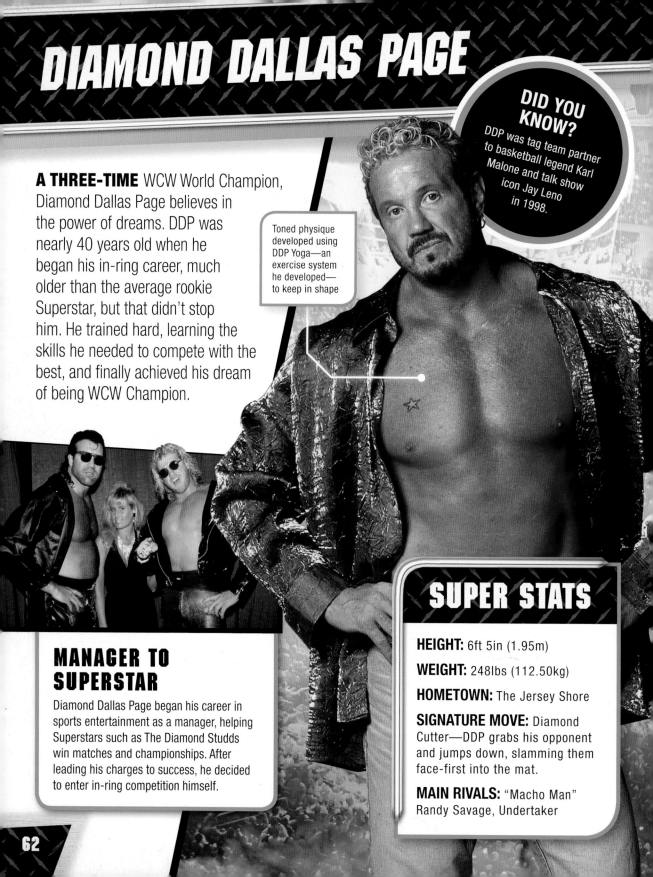

A THREE-TIME WCW World Champion, Diamond Dallas Page believes in the power of dreams. DDP was nearly 40 years old when he began his in-ring career, much older than the average rookie Superstar, but that didn't stop him. He trained hard, learning the skills he needed to compete with the best, and finally achieved his dream of being WCW Champion.

Toned physique developed using DDP Yoga—an exercise system he developed—to keep in shape

MANAGER TO SUPERSTAR

Diamond Dallas Page began his career in sports entertainment as a manager, helping Superstars such as The Diamond Studds win matches and championships. After leading his charges to success, he decided to enter in-ring competition himself.

SUPER STATS

HEIGHT: 6ft 5in (1.95m)

WEIGHT: 248lbs (112.50kg)

HOMETOWN: The Jersey Shore

SIGNATURE MOVE: Diamond Cutter—DDP grabs his opponent and jumps down, slamming them face-first into the mat.

MAIN RIVALS: "Macho Man" Randy Savage, Undertaker

D-LO BROWN

WITH A BOB of his head, D-Lo Brown fired up the crowd and let everyone know he was ready for action. A chest injury early on in Brown's career left him wearing a chest protector during matches. The protector handily increased the impact of his signature move: Lo Down. This, combined with his confidence to the point of arrogance, helped him win the WWE European and Intercontinental Championships.

Nation of Domination faction colors displayed on ring gear

NATION OF DOMINATION

D-Lo Brown debuted in WWE as a member of the Nation of Domination. This faction also included Superstars The Rock, Ron Simmons, and the Godfather.

SUPER STATS

HEIGHT: 6ft 1in (1.85m)

WEIGHT: 277lbs (125.65kg)

HOMETOWN: Las Vegas, Nevada

SIGNATURE MOVE: Lo Down—D-Lo dives off the top rope, pumping his arms and legs in midair before crashing on top of his opponent.

MAIN RIVALS: Raven, D-Generation X

DOLPH ZIGGLER

ZIGGLER IS AN extremely talented Superstar, and he knows it. The former World Heavyweight Champion brags about his abilities and backs them up in the ring. Being a show-off can turn people off, but for Dolph Ziggler, it's had the opposite effect. He has earned the adoration of the WWE Universe. Despite his talent and résumé, Ziggler feels he's been overlooked for title opportunities and that makes him want to show off even more!

DID YOU KNOW?

Early on in his career, Ziggler was part of an all-male cheerleading stable named the Spirit Squad.

MIZ-ERY

After he was drafted to *SmackDown Live*, Ziggler set his sights on The Miz's Intercontinental Championship. The rivals had several matches, but Ziggler finally defeated The Miz for the Title at *No Mercy 2016*.

Flashy gear is all part of Ziggler's "show off" image

SUPER STATS

HEIGHT: 6ft (1.82m)

WEIGHT: 218lbs (99kg)

HOMETOWN: Hollywood, Florida

SIGNATURE MOVE: The Zig Zag —Ziggler grabs his opponent from behind, jumps and pulls them down to the mat by their head.

MAIN RIVALS: The Miz, Baron Corbin

DON MURACO

WITH TOTAL ARROGANCE and a complete disregard for the WWE rulebook, the original "Rock," Don Muraco, was despised throughout his career by the WWE Universe. But while some Superstars might have been distracted by such disdain, Muraco never let it bother him. In fact, he used it to motivate him, enjoying riling up the crowd against him. He became two-time Intercontinental Champion and was inducted into the WWE Hall of Fame in 2004.

Anti-smoking message "No ifs, ands, or butts."

CLASHES WITH BACKLUND

Muraco wanted the WWE Championship. To get it, he had to defeat the champion, Bob Backlund. Their 60-minute matches became instant classics, though Muraco never won the Title.

Taping his thumb made Muraco's Asian Spike move more devastating than ever

SUPER STATS

HEIGHT: 6ft 3in (1.90m)

WEIGHT: 275lbs (124.73kg)

HOMETOWN: Sunset Beach, Hawaii

SIGNATURE MOVE: Asian Spike —Muraco jabs his thumb into his opponent.

MAIN RIVALS: Ricky "The Dragon" Steamboat, Bob Backlund

DREW GULAK

THIS SUPERSTAR prides himself on being tough. Gulak doesn't wear knee or elbow pads when he competes in the ring—he believes they are unnecessary and are only worn by weaker Superstars! He has a conservative, technical ring style that focuses on submission holds and mat grappling, and he criticises fellow cruiserweights when they use flashier moves. Gulak hopes his approach will get him the WWE Cruiserweight Championship.

Megaphone helps spread the message that high-flying moves are too dangerous

Sharp suit for a straight-to-business approach

STUDENT OF THE GAME

Drew Gulak is a "student of the game," meaning he studies great matches from WWE history. He learns from technical wizards such as Mr. Perfect and Shawn Michaels.

SUPER STATS

HEIGHT: 6ft (1.82m)

WEIGHT: 193lbs (87.54kg)

HOMETOWN: Philadelphia, Pennsylvania

SIGNATURE MOVE: Dragon Sleeper —Gulak grabs his opponent from behind, drags them to the mat, and wraps his legs around their waist.

MAIN RIVALS: Rich Swann, Cedric Alexander

DUSTY RHODES

NO WWE SUPERSTAR embodied their nickname more than "The American Dream," Dusty Rhodes. Growing up the poor son of a plumber, Rhodes found great success in sports entertainment. As a hard-working common man, Rhodes connected with the WWE Universe who saw themselves in him and celebrated his victories as their own. Rhodes left a lasting legacy in WWE that includes his son, Goldust, and the hundreds of Superstars he guided as a coach in NXT.

> **DID YOU KNOW?**
> Rhodes's life and career have been honored with a 2009 WWE Hall of Fame induction, and the annual NXT Dusty Rhodes Tag Team Classic tournament.

> Cowboy hat worn at all times

WORLD HEAVYWEIGHT CHAMPION

Created in 1905, the NWA World Heavyweight Championship was the very first championship in sports entertainment. Dusty Rhodes reached the apex of sports entertainment in the 1980s by winning the title three times.

SUPER STATS

HEIGHT: 6ft 2in (1.87m)

WEIGHT: 275lbs (124.73kg)

HOMETOWN: Austin, Texas

SIGNATURE MOVE: Bionic Elbow —Rhodes rolls his elbow back and slams it into the forehead of his opponent.

MAIN RIVALS: Ric Flair, "Million Dollar Man" Ted DiBiase

EDDIE GUERRERO

HE'D LIE, CHEAT, AND STEAL

to win matches and championships, yet Eddie Guerrero was one of the most beloved WWE Superstars to ever set foot in the ring. A member of one of sports entertainment's most influential families in Mexico, Guerrero learned about in-ring competition from his father, Gory Guerrero. It became his greatest passion. He won more than a dozen championships in ECW, WCW, and WWE. Eddie was inducted into the WWE Hall of Fame in 2006.

WINNING THE TITLE

To say Eddie Guerrero was the underdog in his WWE Championship Match against the mammoth Brock Lesnar at *No Way Out 2004* would be an understatement. Yet Guerrero overcame his larger opponent and pinned him to win the Title.

Flames represent Guerrero's passion for competition, which he called "Latino Heat"

SUPER STATS

HEIGHT: 5ft 8in (1.72m)

WEIGHT: 220lbs (99.79kg)

HOMETOWN: El Paso, Texas

SIGNATURE MOVE: Frog Splash— Guerrero leaps from the top rope, extends and retracts his arms and legs, and lands atop his opponent.

MAIN RIVALS: Brock Lesnar, Kurt Angle

EDGE

DID YOU KNOW?

Less than one year after retiring from the ring, Edge was inducted into the WWE Hall of Fame in 2012.

HE'S BEEN CALLED "The Master Manipulator" because of his ability to exploit shortcuts to gain success, but to Edge it's all about making the right decisions at the right time. Taking the nickname "The Rated-R Superstar" because of his vicious mean streak in the ring, Edge proved his brilliance by winning the first-ever Money in the Bank Ladder Match. He then cashed in the Money in the Bank briefcase and won the WWE Title from John Cena.

Sun tattoo is logo for Edge's talk show segment on WWE TV named *The Cutting Edge*

GIVING TLC

Heart-stopping performances made Edge synonymous with Tables, Ladders, and Chairs Matches. The first of these types of matches occurred at *WrestleMania 2000*, where Edge performed his Spear move on Jeff Hardy, off a ladder.

SUPER STATS

HEIGHT: 6ft 5in (1.95m)

WEIGHT: 241lbs (109.31kg)

HOMETOWN: Toronto, Ontario, Canada

SIGNATURE MOVE: Spear—Edge leaps toward his opponent, tackling them around the waist, and driving them to the mat.

MAIN RIVALS: John Cena, Undertaker

ELIAS

DID YOU KNOW?
After being defeated in his Loser Leaves Town Match in NXT, Elias tried sneaking back into NXT wearing a mask and calling himself "El Vagabundo!"

WITH HIS TRUSTY GUITAR always within reach, Elias wanders aimlessly through WWE. Never one to stay in one place for too long, Elias can be found sitting in the ring, strumming his six-string and singing a song about whatever town he happens to be in (and usually insulting the local WWE Universe). But when it's time to compete, "The Drifter" battles his opponents like he's got nothing to lose.

Long hair—Elias is never in one place long enough to get a haircut

LOSER LEAVES TOWN

Elias was challenged to a "Loser Leaves Town" match by Kassius Ohno. Although he fought hard, Elias lost the match and was required to leave NXT. He didn't go far, though. He showed up on *RAW* a few weeks later.

Guitar is Elias's only lifelong friend

SUPER STATS

HEIGHT: 6ft (1.82m)

WEIGHT: 217lbs (98.4kg)

HOMETOWN: Pittsburgh, Pennsylvania

SIGNATURE MOVE: The Encore —Samson pulls his opponent in close under his arm, and spins them up to his shoulder, dropping to the mat.

MAIN RIVALS: Kassius Ohno, Apollo Crews

EMBER MOON

EMERGING FROM THE

shadows like a wolf, Ember Moon competes in the NXT women's division with great strength and agility. She hits hard and fast, striking with catlike precision. Her Eclipse signature move is so devastating that two of its victims, Billie Kay and Peyton Royce, unsuccessfully lobbied NXT General Manager William Regal to ban it! Like the hunter she is, Moon has her eyes set on the ultimate prize: the NXT Women's Championship.

Eye color changes for matches

TWO WARRIORS

Neither Ember Moon nor her opponent at *NXT TakeOver. Orlando*, Asuka, had lost a match in NXT. Moon was determined to end Asuka's winning streak and take her NXT Women's Championship. Although Moon came up short, the match was an impressive battle between the two women.

SUPER STATS

HEIGHT: 5ft 11in (1.80m)

HOMETOWN: Dallas, Texas

SIGNATURE MOVE: The Eclipse—Moon grabs her opponent in a front facelock and, twisting, slams them to the mat.

MAIN RIVALS: Billie Kay, Peyton Royce

EMMA

ONCE KNOWN FOR her bubbly personality (she was actually surrounded by bubbles during her entrance to the ring), Emma has chosen to pursue a darker path. Being fun-loving might have made the WWE Universe like her, but it wasn't bringing her any success in the ring, so she let her more aggressive side come out. Now, the angry Australian has all her fury focused on the *RAW* Women's Championship.

Dark lip color to match her dark personality

REVENGE ON *RAW*

The night after losing a 10-woman tag team match at *WrestleMania 32*, Emma made Becky Lynch, who had been part of the winning team, her primary target. As the underdog in the match, Emma shocked the WWE Universe by defeating Lynch live on *RAW*.

SUPER STATS

HEIGHT: 5ft 5in (1.65m)

HOMETOWN: Melbourne, Australia

SIGNATURE MOVE: Emma Lock —Lies on her opponent's back and pulls up on her head and legs.

MAIN RIVALS: Dana Brooke, Asuka

ENZO AMORE

WITH RAZOR-SHARP wit and a blistering vocabulary of insults, the "Smack Talker Skywalker," as he is often called, has cut down to size some of the biggest and baddest Superstars. Enzo Amore may not be the biggest Superstar in the world, especially compared to his former tag team partner Big Cass, but he doesn't care. Enzo is quick-footed, determined, and ready to beat anyone who stands in his way.

Nothing says "Certified G and Bonafide Stud" more than leopard print

Gold chain shows the world that Enzo is all about glitz and glamour

CERTIFIED G

Enzo famously introduced himself alongside his now estranged partner by saying: "My name is Enzo Amore, and I am a Certified G, and a Bonafide Stud and you can't teach that… Badaboom, realest guy in the room!"

SUPER STATS

HEIGHT: 5ft 11in (1.80m)

WEIGHT: 200lbs (90.71kg)

HOMETOWN: Hackensack, New Jersey

SIGNATURE MOVE: Air Enzo—Enzo dives from the top rope, sometimes propelled by his tag team partner Big Cass, and lands on his opponent.

MAIN RIVALS: Gallows and Anderson, Big Cass

ERIC YOUNG

Upside down bird is a frightening image of anarchy

DID YOU KNOW? Months before forming SAnitY, Eric Young made an appearance in NXT and unsuccessfully challenged Samoa Joe for the NXT Championship.

CHAOS, ANARCHY, and unrest. These are the words that follow Eric Young. A veteran of sports entertainment around the world, Young joined NXT intent on creating chaos to the level of destruction. With his like-minded followers in the SAnitY stable beside him, Young goes in for sneak attacks on random Superstars and acts with reckless abandon inside the ring. No one in NXT is safe from Eric Young's evil designs.

INSANITY

Young recruited Superstars Alexander Wolfe, Killian Dain, and Nikki Cross to form the SAnitY stable. They had one aim: to create chaos in NXT.

SUPER STATS

HEIGHT: 5ft 11in (1.80m)

WEIGHT: 232lbs (105kg)

HOMETOWN: Nashville, Tennessee

SIGNATURE MOVE: Youngblood—Young grabs his opponent by the legs, tosses them in the air, catches them around the neck, and slams them down.

MAIN RIVALS: Tye Dillinger, No Way Jose

ERICK ROWAN

Beard typically featured on members of the Wyatt Family

ONE OF THE DARK

souls that came to WWE with Bray Wyatt's Wyatt Family, Erick Rowan was the family's strongman and intimidator. Rowan struck fear into any who dared cross the Wyatt Family. He has been set free by his "father" and plans to intimidate Superstars on his own terms. With his impressive strength and ability to perform aerial maneuvers, Rowan is a dangerous adversary.

Sheep mask is a scary accessory

LOST SHEEP

Erick Rowan is known for his creepy sheep masks. Originally, they were simply white, but now Rowan makes the masks even creepier by painting them like a clown, or by adding elements from a gas mask.

SUPER STATS

HEIGHT: 6ft 8in (2.03m)

WEIGHT: 315lbs (142.88kg)

HOMETOWN: Minneapolis, Minnesota

SIGNATURE MOVE: The Way —Rowan hoists his opponent up by the legs, and drops them behind him.

MAIN RIVALS: Luke Harper, The New Day

EVE

BRILLIANT, BEAUTIFUL, AND CUNNING, Eve is the ultimate contender. She joined WWE by winning the 2007 Diva Search competition for Superstars and immediately made the WWE Diva's Championship her goal. She won the Title on three occasions, using her impressive athletic ability and sharp mind to defeat her opponents.

Friendly smile often hides a cunning plan

DIVAS CHAMPION
Eve won her first of three Divas Championships by defeating Maryse on *RAW* in 2010. Maryse set Eve up for what appeared to be Maryse's signature move "The French Kiss," but Eve sneakily reversed it into a pin.

SUPER STATS

HEIGHT: 5ft 8in (1.72m)

HOMETOWN: Denver, Colorado

SIGNATURE MOVE: Evesault —Eve does a back flip off the top rope, landing on her opponent.

MAIN RIVALS: Natalya, Brie Bella

FINLAY

HIS NAME IS Finlay, and he loves to fight. And Finlay has been doing just that! After spending two decades competing in matches in Europe, Finlay moved to America where he became a WCW Superstar, competing for the WCW Television and Hardcore Championships. He later joined WWE and fulfilled one of his greatest achievements: winning the United States Championship. Finlay retired from competition in 2012.

Shamrock on ring gear shows pride in his Irish heritage

"Shillelagh," an Irish walking stick, which Finlay frequently used as a weapon

A MEMBER OF THE COURT

Finlay was a member of "King Booker's Court" alongside William Regal. The two Superstars served as knighted bodyguards who protected King Booker from his enemies.

SUPER STATS

HEIGHT: 6ft 2in (1.87m)

WEIGHT: 233lbs (105.68kg)

HOMETOWN: Belfast, Northern Ireland

SIGNATURE MOVE: The Celtic Cross—Finlay lifts his opponent onto his shoulders in a modified fireman's carry and drops backward, landing on them.

MAIN RIVALS: Booker T, William Regal

FINN BÁLOR

DID YOU KNOW?

Finn Bálor was crowned the first-ever WWE Universal Champion after pinning Seth Rollins at SummerSlam 2016.

HE CALLS HIS supporters the Bálor Club, and those enthusiastic club members can be found worldwide. Finn Bálor made his name competing in Ireland and Japan before entering WWE. He made an impact in NXT by becoming the longest-reigning NXT Champion before *RAW* General Manager, Mick Foley recognized Bálor's talent in the 2016 Brand Extension Draft and signed him to *RAW*.

Elaborate headdress is removed before competing

THE DEMON KING

For his biggest matches, Finn Bálor channels his dormant demon within. He covers himself in gruesome body paint and becomes The Demon King—a more aggressive, driven version of himself.

SUPER STATS

HEIGHT: 5ft 11in (1.80m)

WEIGHT: 190lbs (86kg)

HOMETOWN: Bray, County Wicklow, Ireland

SIGNATURE MOVE: Coup de Grace —Bálor jumps off the top rope and stomps on his opponent.

MAIN RIVALS: Bray Wyatt, Kevin Owens

GALLOWS AND ANDERSON

WITH BAD ATTITUDES and more than their fair share of aggression, Luke Gallows and Karl Anderson came to WWE to prove they were the best tag team in the world. They attacked The Usos on their first night on *RAW* and from then on, no other WWE tag teams were safe. This included Cesaro and Sheamus who lost the RAW Tag Team Championship to Gallows and Anderson at the 2017 *Royal Rumble*.

"The Club" logo emblazoned on Luke's shirt

THE CLUB

Gallows and Anderson were allies with AJ Styles during their time competing in Japan. Once all three Superstars signed with WWE they reunited, forming a stable named "The Club" with its own "Too Sweet" hand sign.

SUPER STATS

NAMES: Luke Gallows, Karl Anderson

COMBINED WEIGHT: 505lbs (229.06kg)

SIGNATURE MOVE: Magic Killer —Gallows and Anderson lift their opponent onto their shoulders in a bridge between them and spin them off and onto the ground.

MAIN RIVALS: The New Day, The Hardy Boyz

GEORGE "THE ANIMAL" STEELE

FOR SOMEONE WITH the nickname "The Animal," Steele was surprisingly gentle, most of the time. However, many felt the full force of his aggression when they made him angry. Steele was known for his trademark green tongue and hairy body. He spoke very few words, and grunted to express himself. Steele also liked to dine on the turnbuckle pad in the corner of the ring, gnawing it open with his teeth and using the remains as a weapon!

"Mine," Steele's cuddly toy, was the Superstar's regular companion to the ring

A LITTLE CRUSH

Steele developed a crush on "Macho Man" Randy Savage's manager, Miss Elizabeth, which angered Savage. Though Elizabeth was flattered and Steele was kind to her, Savage made sure Steele never got too close!

SUPER STATS

HEIGHT: 6ft 1in (1.85m)

WEIGHT: 275lbs (124.73kg)

HOMETOWN: Detroit, Michigan

SIGNATURE MOVE: Flying Hammerlock—Steele would twist his opponent's arm behind him and hoist them into the air.

MAIN RIVALS: "Macho Man" Randy Savage, Bruno Sammartino

FOLLOWED TO THE

ring by beautiful women, the Godfather was a happy-go-lucky Superstar who loved WWE. The WWE Universe, in turn, loved him, cheering with incredible excitement every time he came to the ring. When the came time to compete, The Godfather was serious and focused. The popular Superstar became Tag Team and Intercontinental Champion and was honored with an induction into the WWE Hall of Fame in 2016.

Gold jewelry helps make the Godfather look flashy

THE GOODFATHER

Calling himself "the Goodfather" and wearing a shirt and tie, the Godfather joined "Right to Censor," a stable of Superstars who felt that WWE had become inappropriate for children. He competed against Superstars such as D-Von Dudley of The Dudley Boyz, but he very quickly returned to being the Godfather.

SUPER STATS

HEIGHT: 6ft 6in (1.98m)

WEIGHT: 330lbs (149.68kg)

HOMETOWN: Las Vegas, Nevada

SIGNATURE MOVE: Big Splash —Godfather jumps from the mat and lands on his opponent.

MAIN RIVAL: Undertaker

DID YOU KNOW?

Goldberg won the WCW World Heavyweight Championship in his hometown Atlanta, Georgia in front of 60,000 fans—the largest non-pay-per-view crowd in history.

Goldberg's tattoo doubles as his logo

BEGINNING WITH HIS

WCW debut in 1997, Goldberg became one of the most powerful and dominant Superstars in sports entertainment history. A former WCW, World Heavyweight, and WWE Universal Champion, Goldberg has beaten the biggest names in WWE, including The Rock and Triple H. After a 12-year break, Goldberg returned to WWE in 2016 to challenge Brock Lesnar to a match at *Survivor Series*, defeating him in one minute and 26 seconds.

Gloves protect hands from hard punches

THE STREAK

Goldberg's very first match was against WCW Superstar Hugh Morrus on *WCW Monday Nitro* in 1997. Goldberg's victory was the start of his record-breaking undefeated streak of 173 matches.

SUPER STATS

HEIGHT: 6ft 4in (1.93m)

WEIGHT: 285lbs (129kg)

HOMETOWN: Atlanta, Georgia

SIGNATURE MOVE: Jackhammer—Goldberg lifts his opponent by the head, legs in the air, curls their body around him, and slams them to the mat.

MAIN RIVALS: Brock Lesnar, Kevin Owens

GOLDUST

YOU'LL NEVER FORGET the name Goldust—that's the promise this Superstar makes to the WWE Universe. Goldust fancies himself a brilliant filmmaker, but it's in the ring where he displays his true talent. To his opponents, Goldust, also known as "The Bizarre One," is an unpredictable competitor in the ring. His methodical and hard-hitting style helped him capture the Intercontinental Championship and the WWE Tag Team Championship on three occasions.

Face paint changes for each match appearance

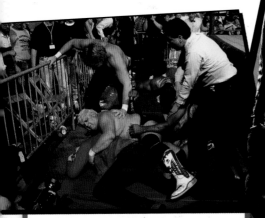

FAMILY BACKUP

Before breaking out on his own and covering himself with gold leaf, Dustin teamed up with his dad, WWE Hall of Famer Dusty Rhodes, to battle "Million Dollar Man" Ted DiBiase and DiBiase's manservant, Virgil.

SUPER STATS

HEIGHT: 6ft 6in (1.98m)

WEIGHT: 232lbs (105kg)

HOMETOWN: Hollywood, California

SIGNATURE MOVE: Curtain Call —Goldust grabs his opponent around the neck from behind, bends him backward, lifts him up, and slams him down on his back.

MAIN RIVALS: R-Truth, Razor Ramon

THE GOON

ICE HOCKEY might be considered a violent sport, but The Goon was too aggressive even for that game. He had spent more time in the penalty box than on the ice, and was banned for fighting. So, he made his way to WWE where he could unleash the full force of his violent ways on his rivals. He declared he would be WWE's "scoring king" when it came to in-ring competition.

Hockey gear worn as ring gear

BIG RETURN

The Goon competed in WWE for less than a year in 1996, but he returned to compete in a special Battle Royal at *WrestleMania X-7* in 2001—his first appearance at a *WrestleMania* event.

Gloves are dropped before battling in the ring

SUPER STATS

HEIGHT: 6ft 1in (1.85m)

WEIGHT: 250lbs (113.39kg)

HOMETOWN: Duluth, Minnesota

SIGNATURE MOVE: Cross-Check—The Goon runs full force into the back of his opponent, knocking them to the mat.

MAIN RIVALS: Undertaker, The Stalker

GORILLA MONSOON

FOLLOWING A LEGENDARY

in-ring career that saw him challenge the likes of Bruno Sammartino, André the Giant, and even boxing's greatest, Muhammed Ali, who jumped into the ring during one of his matches in 1976, Gorilla Monsoon settled behind the microphone and became the iconic voice of WWE. He became a commentator on nearly every WWE program and pay-per-view event for the next 15 years. He enhanced every match with his excited, passionate style.

Fists used to show passion, never to confront Superstars

MR. PRESIDENT

In 1995, Gorilla Monsoon was appointed President of WWE. In his new role, he planned matches, enforced WWE rules, and disciplined WWE Superstars when needed—including challenging rule-breaking Superstar Vader.

SUPER STATS

HEIGHT: 6ft 7in (2.01m)

WEIGHT: 401lbs (181.89kg)

HOMETOWN: Manchuria

SIGNATURE MOVE: Airplane Spin—Monsoon lifts his opponent onto his shoulders in a fireman's carry and spins around.

MAIN RIVALS: Bruno Sammartino, André the Giant

GRAN METALIK

DID YOU KNOW?

Gran Metalik's name can be loosely translated as "Heavy Metal."

BEING INVITED TO WWE as part of the 2016 Cruiserweight Classic tournament was a great honor for Gran Metalik. Having honed his in-ring skills in Mexico, Metalik proved to be a major player in the tournament. He defeated four other cruiserweight Superstars to advance to the tournament finals. Although he lost the final match against TJP, Metalik was able to showcase his amazing talent.

Disguise, matched with high-flying moves, makes Metalik look like a superhero

KING OF THE ROPES

Gran Metalik uses amazing aerial maneuvers in his matches, like his high-flying Moonsault move. His soaring skills earned him the nickname "El Rey de las Cuerdas," which translates to "The King of the Ropes."

SUPER STATS

HEIGHT: 5ft 9in (1.75m)

WEIGHT: 175lbs (79.38kg)

HOMETOWN: Guadalajara, Jalisco, Mexico

SIGNATURE MOVE: Metalik Driver—Metalik lifts his opponent onto his shoulders, jumps and drops them down again.

MAIN RIVALS: TJP, Drew Gulak

HACKSAW JIM DUGGAN

WITH THE AMERICAN

flag in one hand and his trusty two-by-four piece of wood in the other, "Hacksaw" Jim Duggan entered his matches with the same plan: Attack, attack, attack! The former professional football player had a rough and tumble in-ring style, and loved yelling out his battle cry, "Hooooooo!" and leading the WWE Universe in chants of "USA!" during matches.

2x4 piece of wood rarely used as a weapon—despite being brought to every match

DREAM TITLE

There was no better title win for the patriotic Superstar than the United States Championship. Duggan won the Title during his time competing in WCW in 1994.

SUPER STATS

HEIGHT: 6ft 3in (1.90m)

WEIGHT: 270lbs (122.47kg)

HOMETOWN: Glens Falls, New York

SIGNATURE MOVE: Three Point Stance Clothesline—Duggan squats down into football's three point stance and runs toward his opponent, smashing them with his outstretched arm.

MAIN RIVALS: Diamond Dallas Page, Sgt. Slaughter

THE HARDY BOYZ

FROM THE TIME they debuted in WWE in 1998, The Hardy Boyz have been embraced by the WWE Universe. Known for risky maneuvers such as diving off high platforms and ladders, The Hardyz are seven-time Tag Team Champions in WWE. They left WWE in 2010 but made a surprising return at *WrestleMania 33*, where they won the *RAW* Tag Team Championship in a Four-way Ladder Match.

Ear gauge part of Jeff's "extreme" look

DOUBLE SUCCESS

Beyond their legendary success as a tag team, Jeff and Matt have also had incredible success in singles competition. In 2008, they were both in peak position: Jeff was WWE Champion and Matt was ECW Champion.

SUPER STATS

NAMES: Jeff Hardy, Matt Hardy

COMBINED WEIGHT: 461lbs (209.11kg)

HOMETOWN: Cameron, North Carolina

SIGNATURE MOVE: Twist of Fate/ Swanton Bomb—Matt grabs their opponent and swings them down to the mat as Jeff dives off the top rope, flips in the air, and lands on the opponent.

MAIN RIVALS: Cesaro and Sheamus, Gallows and Anderson

HARLEY RACE

WITH SEVEN World Heavyweight Championship wins on his résumé, "The Handsome One," as Harley Race liked to be called, makes a solid case for his claim that he was once the greatest Superstar on Earth. Known for being tough as nails with his rugged in-ring approach, Race defeated several WWE Hall of Famers, including Ric Flair and Dusty Rhodes, on his way to world championship glory.

Blond locks make Race particularly handsome

KING OF THE RING

Race won the 1986 *King of the Ring* tournament, henceforth calling himself "King Harley Race." Wearing a crown and long purple cape, Race issued proclamations challenging his rivals to matches and demanding respect from the WWE Universe.

SUPER STATS

HEIGHT: 6ft 1in (1.85m)

WEIGHT: 253lbs (114.76kg)

HOMETOWN: Kansas City, Missouri

SIGNATURE MOVE: Piledriver —Race holds his opponent upside down and drops them downward to the mat.

MAIN RIVALS: Ric Flair, Junkyard Dog

HEATH SLATER

"THE ONE MAN BAND," as Heath Slater likes to be called, refers to Slater's mistaken belief that he's a rockstar who doesn't need help defeating other Superstars. He is a frequent underdog who is outsized in the ring. Slater's boasts often get him in trouble with his opponents and his tag team partner, Rhyno, gets him out of tough situations.

T-shirt reminds everyone how badly Slater needs his job as a Superstar

"I GOT KIDS!"

Slater wasn't drafted by either *RAW* or *SmackDown Live* during the 2016 Brand Extension Draft. Disappointed, Slater lobbied *SmackDown Live* Commissioner Shane McMahon and reminded him "I got kids!" His efforts were rewarded and he was signed to *SmackDown Live*.

SUPER STATS

HEIGHT: 6ft 2in (1.87m)

WEIGHT: 216lbs (97.90kg)

HOMETOWN: Pineville, West Virginia

SIGNATURE MOVE: Smash Hit—Slater picks his opponent up by the waist and slams them to the mat.

MAIN RIVALS: Diamond Dallas Page, The Wyatt Family

HEAVY MACHINERY

ROOKIES TO WWE, Otis Dozovic and Tucker Knight are hoping to be a massive destructive force in the NXT tag team division. They have a lot to prove as one of the newest tag teams to join NXT. But don't mistake inexperience for weakness. They are built machine-tough, and are determined to make a name for themselves by demolishing the competition and capturing the NXT Tag Team Championship.

Warning signs remind their opponents to be cautious

HEAVY MACHINERY

POWERFUL START

One of Heavy Machinery's first matches in NXT was against Mike Marshall and Jonathan Ortagun. Showcasing their incredible strength and power, Heavy Machinery worked together to plow over Marshall like the bulldozers they are.

SUPER STATS

NAMES: Otis Dozovic, Tucker Knight

COMBINED WEIGHT: 650lbs (294.80kg)

SIGNATURE MOVE: Boom Shaka Loo—The two members of Heavy Machinery run toward each other, crushing their opponent between them.

MAIN RIVALS: The Revival, Authors of Pain

HIDEO ITAMI

DON'T BE FOOLED by his size —Hideo Itami is one of the hardest-hitting Superstars in NXT. A few months after his signing to WWE, Itami earned a spot in the André the Giant's Memorial Battle Royal at *WrestleMania 31*. Though he didn't win the match, he represented NXT well as its only competing Superstar. Having overcome major injuries, Itami is focused on winning the NXT Championship.

Hands ready to strike so fast, opponents won't see them coming

Scar from a brutal match in Japan

BUSINESS MATTERS

Triple H and Mr. McMahon put pressure on the NXT Superstars by recruiting Itami, one of the biggest stars from Japanese sports entertainment. NXT Superstars will have to up their game to handle Itami's fast-paced moves.

SUPER STATS

HEIGHT: 5ft 9in (1.75m)

WEIGHT: 182lbs (82.5kg)

HOMETOWN: Tokyo, Japan

SIGNATURE MOVE: Go To Sleep —Itami lifts his opponent up onto his shoulders in a fireman's carry, then dumps them down over his head and onto his waiting knee.

MAIN RIVALS: Bobby Roode, Tyler Breeze

HIGH CHIEF PETER MAIVIA

DID YOU KNOW?

Peter Maivia's title of "High Chief" is given to a man who is a great leader of his family and in the governing bodies of Samoa.

MORE RECENTLY KNOWN for being the grandfather of popular Superstar, The Rock, High Chief Peter Maivia is legendary in his own right. Upon joining WWE, Maivia chased the WWE Championship, competing with his greatest rivals Bob Backlund and Superstar Billy Graham. Though unsuccessful in winning the championship, Maivia received his greatest honor when he was posthumously inducted into the WWE Hall of Fame by The Rock in 2008.

Maivia's tattoos cover his legs up to his waist

SUPERSTAR FAMILY

There have been several WWE Superstars who are members of the Anoa'i Family, including High Chief Peter Maivia, The Wild Samoans, Yokozuna, Roman Reigns, The Rock, The Usos, Nia Jax, and Rikishi.

SUPER STATS

HEIGHT: 5ft 9in (1.75m)

WEIGHT: 275lbs (124.73kg)

HOMETOWN: The Isle of Samoa

SIGNATURE MOVE: Stump Puller —with his opponent seated on the mat, Maivia sits behind them and pulls their legs up toward their chest.

MAIN RIVALS: Bob Backlund, "Superstar" Billy Graham

HONKY TONK MAN

THE HONKY TONK MAN believed that he was ten times the rock-and-roll star Elvis Presley was. While that is up for debate, The Honky Tonk Man's ability in the ring was indisputable. He would often dance and play a song on his trusty guitar before getting down to business in the ring. His dance-inspired moves made quick work of his opponents and he had a mean streak that he displayed frequently against his competitors.

SUPER STATS

HEIGHT: 6ft 1in (1.85m)

WEIGHT: 243lbs (110.22kg)

HOMETOWN: Memphis, Tennessee

SIGNATURE MOVE: Shake, Rattle, and Roll—Honky Tonk Man grabs his opponent face down under one arm, grabs their arm and spins backward, slamming them back onto the mat.

MAIN RIVALS: Ricky "The Dragon" Steamboat, Ultimate Warrior

KING OF THE WINS

The Honky Tonk Man may not be the king of rock and roll, but he does hold the record for the longest reign as WWE Intercontinental Champion. He was champion for 454 days before losing the Title to Ultimate Warrior at *SummerSlam 1988.*

Guitar primarily used as a musical instrument, but also a weapon during matches

HOWARD FINKEL

Some Superstars are known for their strength; Finkel is known for his golden voice

NICKNAMED "THE FINK,"

Howard Finkel is one of the best-known ring announcers in WWE history. Finkel has seen it all. He has served as ring announcer for countless matches, his voice echoing in arenas and stadiums with his trademark, "And nneeewwwwww…" when a new Superstar captures a championship. In 2009, Finkel was the first announcer to be inducted into the WWE Hall of Fame.

DID YOU KNOW?
Finkel is the WWE Superstar with the most appearances at WrestleMania, having appeared a total of 32 years.

Tuxedo is Finkel's attire of choice, whether announcing or competing in matches

TUXEDO MATCH

Finkel occasionally stepped into the ring to take matters into his own hands. He battled and defeated manager Harvey Wippleman, who'd been bullying him, by removing his tuxedo in a Tuxedo Match in 1995.

SUPER STATS

HOMETOWN: Newark, New Jersey

KEY MOMENT: Finkel served as X-Pac's manager in a Hair vs. Hair Match at *SummerSlam* 1998

MAIN RIVALS: Harvey Wippleman, Lilian Garcia

IRON SHEIK

Traditional headdress called a "keffiyeh"

DID YOU KNOW?
At WrestleMania X-Seven, the Iron Sheik entered and won a legends' battle royal, 18 years after having won the WWE Championship!

A TRAINED GRAPPLER from Iran, The Iron Sheik joined WWE and immediately embarked on a mission to prove his dominance. Confronting Superstars such as Sgt. Slaughter, the Iron Sheik used whatever underhanded tactics he could—including eye rakes, powder throwing, and low blows—to gain victories. He soon joined forces with Nikolai Volkoff, winning the WWE Tag Team Championship.

Name of homeland displayed proudly on his ring gear

CHAMPION OF THE WORLD

In December 1983, The Iron Sheik defeated Bob Backlund to become WWE Champion. The Iron Sheik celebrated his win as a victory for Iran.

SUPER STATS

HEIGHT: 6ft (1.82m)

WEIGHT: 258lbs (117.02kg)

HOMETOWN: Tehran, Iran

SIGNATURE MOVE: Camel Clutch—Iron Sheik sits on his opponent's back and pulls their head and shoulders back in a painful submission move.

MAIN RIVALS: Sgt. Slaughter, Bob Backlund

IRWIN R. SCHYSTER

WITH NO TOLERANCE FOR anyone who cheats on their taxes (even though he cheats in his matches), Irwin R. Schyster, or IRS as he's better known, threatens his fellow Superstars with in-ring punishment for their violations. A skilled and savvy technician in the ring, IRS calculates the best strategies to use to defeat his opponents, and brings them down like a tax auditor in a fraud case.

Glasses worn when studying tax audits and devising ways to beat opponents

Superstars' tax records stored in a briefcase that is also a handy weapon in matches

MONEY, INC.

IRS joined forces with another financially focused Superstar, "Million Dollar Man" Ted DiBiase, to form the tag team "Money, Inc." The team saw great success, winning the WWE Tag Team Championship on three occasions in 1992 and 1993.

SUPER STATS

HEIGHT: 6ft 3in (1.90m)

WEIGHT: 248lbs (112.50kg)

HOMETOWN: Washington, D.C.

SIGNATURE MOVE: The Write Off—IRS bounces off the ropes and leaps into the air toward their opponent, hitting them with a vicious flying clothesline.

MAIN RIVALS: Big Boss Man, Tatanka

97

JACK GALLAGHER

EXTREMELY POLITE, exquisitely presented and incomparably competitive, "Gentleman" Jack Gallagher brings a high level of class to the WWE cruiserweight division. He is a proud Englishman who has made it his goal to become WWE Cruiserweight Champion. To him, it's only a matter of time—he has proven he can escape any hold and counter any move his opponents throw at him.

Well-styled mustache—the mark of a true gentleman

Umbrella named "William III"

FLYING GENTLEMAN

Jack Gallagher is never seen without his trusty umbrella. The umbrella has been used as a weapon in the past, but more frequently Gallagher uses it to fly through the air in spectacular aerial maneuvers.

SUPER STATS

HEIGHT: 5ft 8in (1.72m)

WEIGHT: 167lbs (75.74kg)

HOMETOWN: Manchester, United Kingdom

SIGNATURE MOVE: Running Dropkick—Gallagher runs across the ring and jumps at his opponent, kicking them with both feet.

MAIN RIVALS: Neville, Ariya Daivari

JAKE "THE SNAKE" ROBERTS

DID YOU KNOW?
Jake "The Snake" Roberts helped train Diamond Dallas Page for in-ring competition.

THIS SUPERSTAR IS as cunning and devious as a serpent. Jake "The Snake" Roberts's motto, "never trust a snake," is a wise warning to be heeded by his opponents. A master manipulator, Roberts would attack his opponents psychologically as well as physically. He was known to celebrate his victories by letting his pet snakes slither over his defeated adversaries!

Snake for intimidating opponents

BLINDFOLD MATCH

After temporarily losing his eyesight from being sprayed by Rick "The Model" Martel's perfume, Roberts challenged Martel to a blindfold match at *WrestleMania VII*. With the WWE Universe on his side to guide him, Roberts won the match.

SUPER STATS

HEIGHT: 6ft 6in (1.98m)

WEIGHT: 249lbs (112.94kg)

HOMETOWN: Stone Mountain, Georgia

SIGNATURE MOVE: DDT—Roberts holds his opponent's head face down under his arm and jumps backward, dropping onto the mat.

MAIN RIVALS: Ricky "The Dragon" Steamboat, "Macho Man" Randy Savage

JAMES ELLSWORTH

Baseball cap and hoodie give a "regular guy" image

"ANY MAN WITH two hands has a fighting chance." That's James Ellsworth's motto, and he fights like he means it. His self-belief has driven him to pursue matches with top Superstars such as AJ Styles, even though he may not have the experience to compete. Still, Ellsworth gives every match his personal best, because deep down he knows he has that fighting chance to win.

DID YOU KNOW?

Double trouble? Ellsworth's first WWE match was against Braun Strowman, who is more than twice his size.

Ellsworth named his "no chin" signature move after what some may see as a weak feature

CARMELLSWORTH

Their relationship may baffle some of the WWE Universe, but Ellsworth has become WWE Superstar Carmella's close friend. He supports her through all her matches, and tries to intimidate opponents to give her an extra edge.

SUPER STATS

HEIGHT: 5ft 9in (1.75m)

WEIGHT: 175lbs (79.38kg)

HOMETOWN: Baltimore, Maryland

SIGNATURE MOVE: No Chin Music—Ellsworth bashes his opponents in the chin.

MAIN RIVALS: AJ Styles, Becky Lynch

JASON JORDAN

AFTER WINNING LOTS of championships in collegiate wrestling at Indiana University, Jason Jordan brought tremendous talent and experience to NXT and WWE. A former member of the dominant tag team American Alpha, Jordan joined *RAW* as a singles competitor in 2017. Setting his sights on The Miz's Intercontinental Championship, Jordan is determined to be as successful in singles action as he was in college and tag team competition.

Singlet is in the style of those typically worn by amateur wrestlers

A NEW ANGLE

In the summer of 2017, the WWE Universe was shocked to learn that Jason Jordan was the son of *RAW* General Manager, Kurt Angle. Jordan left his American Alpha tag team partner Chad Gable at *SmackDown Live*, and joined *RAW* to be closer to his father.

SUPER STATS

HEIGHT: 6ft 3in (1.90m)

WEIGHT: 245lbs (111.13kg)

HOMETOWN: Chicago, Illinois

SIGNATURE MOVE: Grand Amplitude—Jordon flips his opponent backward over his head.

MAIN RIVALS: The Miz, Curtis Axel

JERRY "THE KING" LAWLER

THE ONLY KING in the ring? Jerry "The King" Lawler joined WWE in 1992. From then on, Memphis's favorite son has bickered and battled with a long list of Superstars. The same sharp tongue that got him in trouble with rivals helped him become an icon as a commentator. Nearly two decades in the broadcast booth is a truly majestic achievement.

DID YOU KNOW?

Lawler is not just an artist in the ring. His artwork features on the cover of a sports entertainment comic.

Wild t-shirts help Lawler rock the broadcast box

GREATEST HITS

Lawler's most famous rivalry was with Bret "Hit Man" Hart. The duo faced each other in countless matches from 1993 to 1995, exchanging wins and losses and as many stinging insults as smooth moves.

SUPER STATS

HEIGHT: 6ft (1.82m)

WEIGHT: 243lbs (110.22kg)

HOMETOWN: Memphis, Tennessee

SIGNATURE MOVE: Flying Fist Drop—Lawler jumps from the second ring rope, smashing his fist onto his opponent.

MAIN RIVALS: Bret "Hit Man" Hart, Jake "The Snake" Roberts

JIM "THE ANVIL" NEIDHART

ROUGH, TOUGH,

and built like a tank, Jim "The Anvil" Neidhart is a powerhouse whose sheer strength has rarely been matched in WWE. Neidhart got his start in Calgary, Alberta, Canada, where he was trained by WWE Hall of Famer, Stu Hart. He married Hart's daughter, Ellie, and they are parents of WWE Superstar Natalya. Alongside his brother-in-law Bret "Hit Man" Hart, Neidhart is a two-time World Tag Team Champion.

Distinctive beard and wild laugh are Neidhart's trademarks

FAMILY WAY

Before he retired, Neidhart was part of the Hart Foundation. This supergroup was led by Bret "Hit Man" Hart and included his brother-in-law British Bulldog and Brian Pillman, who had been trained by the Hart family.

SUPER STATS

HEIGHT: 6ft 2in (1.87m)

WEIGHT: 281lbs (127.46kg)

HOMETOWN: Reno, Nevada

SIGNATURE MOVE: Anvil Flattener —Neidhart lifts his opponent up to his chest and slams them down to the mat, landing on top of them.

MAIN RIVALS: Nasty Boys, Natural Disasters

JINDER MAHAL

Turban is removed before matches

"DON'T HINDER JINDER!" was the rallying cry from WWE Universe, and Jinder Mahal heard every word. After years of struggling to find success, Mahal set his sights on his ultimate goal: the WWE Championship. He honed his in-ring skills and physical strength until he shocked the world by defeating Randy Orton for the title in May 2017.

TEAMING UP

In 2016, Mahal and Rusev joined forces as a powerhouse tag team supported by Rusev's manager, Lana. The pair split up after Rusev accidentally distracted Mahal in a match against The New Day.

SUPER STATS

HEIGHT: 6ft 5in (1.95m)

WEIGHT: 238lbs (107.96kg)

HOMETOWN: Punjab, India

SIGNATURE MOVE: Khallas—Mahal wraps his arms around the upper portion of his opponent's body and slams them down.

MAIN RIVALS: Randy Orton, Darren Young

JOHN CENA

WHETHER HIS RIVALS like him or not, they know John Cena will show up, give his absolute best, and always do the right thing. All that matters to Cena is being the best. He's been the face of WWE for over a decade, winning championships and beating every Superstar that's sought to challenge him. From his legendary matches against The Rock to his relationship with Nikki Bella, the WWE Universe follows Cena's every move.

Military-style dog tags to show respect for soldiers and their families who make great sacrifices

Cena's motto, "Never Give Up," reminds everyone to persevere and overcome challenges

SIXTEEN-TIME CHAMPION

John Cena defeated AJ Styles at the 2017 *Royal Rumble*, winning his 16th WWE World Championship and tying the record of World Title reigns held by legendary Superstar Ric Flair.

SUPER STATS

HEIGHT: 6ft 1in (1.85m)

WEIGHT: 251lbs (113.85kg)

HOMETOWN: West Newbury, Massachusetts

SIGNATURE MOVE: Attitude Adjustment—Cena lifts his opponent up in a fireman's carry, and flips him down onto the mat.

MAIN RIVALS: The Rock, AJ Styles

JOHNNY GARGANO

GARGANO JOINED NXT with his lifelong best friend Tommaso Ciampa in the first annual Dusty Rhodes Tag Team Invitational tournament. Calling themselves #DIY, they went on to win the NXT Tag Team Championship together. However, Ciampa turned on Gargano and the team broke up. Never one to give up, Gargano is using his new status as a strong-willed singles competitor. Calling himself "Johnny Wrestling," he plans to fight his way to the top of NXT.

Gargano makes up for his small size with fierce determination and plenty of experience

CRUISERWEIGHT CLASSIC

Though still tag team partners, Gargano and Ciampa faced each other in the first round of the Cruiserweight Classic tournament. The Superstars competed in a back-and-forth contest that saw Gargano victorious over Ciampa.

SUPER STATS

HEIGHT: 5ft 10in (1.77m)

WEIGHT: 199lbs (90.30kg)

HOMETOWN: Cleveland, Ohio

SIGNATURE MOVE: Gargano Escape—Gargano wraps his arms around the top of his opponent on the mat and pulls back in a painful submission move.

MAIN RIVALS: Authors of Pain, The Revival

JUNKYARD DOG

APPEARING IN A WWE cartoon series as well as in high-profile matches, Junkyard Dog was a Superstar beloved by the youngest members of the WWE Universe. "JYD," as he was known, brought supporters into the ring to dance with him before or after matches. But his friendly demeanor was a ruse—JYD battled his opponents with tremendous aggression.

DID YOU KNOW?

JYD defeated "Macho Man" Randy Savage in the finals of a 16-man tournament at WWE's first-ever pay-per-view event, *The Wrestling Classic*, in 1985.

Chain and collar occasionally used as a weapon against opponents

WHO'S KING?

King of the Ring, Harley Race, tried to force his opponents to bow before him, but JYD refused to bow before any Superstar. JYD was determined to dethrone Harley Race at *WrestleMania III* and claim his crown. Though Race won the match, JYD got the last laugh by attacking Race post match and stealing his cape and crown.

SUPER STATS

HEIGHT: 6ft 3in (1.90m)

WEIGHT: 280lbs (127kg)

HOMETOWN: Charlotte, North Carolina

SIGNATURE MOVE: "Thump" Powerslam—Junkyard Dog lifts his opponent up to his chest, and leaps down to the mat, landing on top of him.

MAIN RIVALS: Harley Race, "Million Dollar Man" Ted DiBiase

KALISTO

BEHIND THE MASK is a man with incredible speed and unparalleled agility: Kalisto. Whether battling heavyweights in the tag team division or his fellow Cruiserweight Superstars, Kalisto brings passion and energy to every match. He learned the ins and outs of sports entertainment in Mexico, and delights the WWE Universe with his visually stunning matches.

One of Kalisto's dozens of unique masks

Dragon motif on Kalisto's vest is a reference to his tag team, The Lucha Dragons

DRAGON TAG

Kalisto partnered with fellow Superstar Sin Cara to form The Lucha Dragons. The masked marvels beat The Ascension to win the NXT Tag Team Championship in 2014.

SUPER STATS

HEIGHT: 5ft 6in (1.67m)

WEIGHT: 170lbs (77.11kg)

HOMETOWN: Mexico City, Mexico

SIGNATURE MOVE: Salida del Sol— Kalisto stands in front of his opponent, hooks their arms in his, and jumps backward over them, dragging them down as he lands.

MAIN RIVALS: Braun Strowman, Apollo Crews

KANE

UNDERTAKER'S YOUNGER BROTHER

Kane debuted in WWE in 1997 and immediately targeted his sibling. Events in their childhood left them bitter enemies. Despite his years of terrorising WWE, Kane has learned to suppress his evil instincts and fill a corporate role with "The Authority"—Stephanie McMahon and Triple H—as their Director of Operations. With 23 championships under his belt, Kane is the ideal candidate for the job.

Conservative suit and tie for Director role

THE DEVIL'S FAVORITE DEMON

Although usually in control of his demonic impulses, sometimes Kane can't resist them. When he puts his mask on, "The Devil's Favorite Demon" is unleashed, and Kane does horrible things such as setting a casket on fire—with his brother Undertaker inside!

SUPER STATS

HEIGHT: 7ft (2.13m)

WEIGHT: 323lbs (146.51kg)

HOMETOWN: Knoxville, Tennessee

SIGNATURE MOVE: Tombstone —Kane lifts his opponent on his chest and turns them upside down, dropping them down onto the mat.

MAIN RIVALS: Undertaker, Big Show

KASSIUS OHNO

HE'S A HARD-HITTING Superstar who has earned the nickname "The Knockout Artist"—but that's not enough for Kassius Ohno. He won't be satisfied until he wins the NXT Championship. On his first day in NXT, Ohno confronted then champion Shinsuke Nakamura, making his intentions very clear. It's only a matter of time before he reaches his goal.

Protective elbow pads for when Ohno applies his knockout moves

NXT VETERAN

Kassius Ohno was an original NXT Superstar from 2012 to 2013, facing opponents such as William Regal, but he left the company to work on his skills. After a four-year hiatus, Ohno returned to begin his NXT Championship quest.

SUPER STATS

HEIGHT: 6ft 4in (1.93m)

WEIGHT: 270lbs (122.47kg)

HOMETOWN: Dayton, Ohio

SIGNATURE MOVE: Rolling Elbow —Ohno spins in a circle, slamming his elbow into his opponent.

MAIN RIVALS: The Wyatt Family, Elias Samson

KEN SHAMROCK

THE FIRST ATHLETE to cross over from the world of mixed martial arts (MMA) to sports entertainment, Ken Shamrock competed in the ring the same way he did in the octagon—by hitting hard, fast, and with a variety of strikes, kicks, and submission holds. It's easy to see how he got the nickname "The World's Most Dangerous Man." In 1998, this hard-fighting Superstar won the Intercontinental Championship and was crowned King of the Ring.

MMA gear provides extra protection during matches

IN THE LION'S DEN

Shamrock competed in several MMA-style WWE matches. Billed as "Lion's Den" matches, the eight-sided cage bouts were won by Shamrock, including a match at *SummerSlam 99* against Steve Blackman.

SUPER STATS

HEIGHT: 6ft 1in (1.85m)

WEIGHT: 243lbs (110.22kg)

HOMETOWN: Sacramento, California

SIGNATURE MOVE: Ankle Lock —Shamrock grabs his opponent by the ankle and twists it in a painful submission hold.

MAIN RIVALS: Vader, Viscera

KERRY VON ERICH

Headband worn in every match

AS HIS NICKNAME suggests, "The Texas Tornado" Kerry Von Erich made an immediate impact when he arrived in WWE, by snatching the Intercontinental Championship from longtime champion Mr. Perfect. Von Erich had previously made a name for himself as an NWA World Heavyweight Champion. He was also the centerpiece of WCCW, his family's sports entertainment company.

THE VON ERICHS

Kerry was the only Von Erich to compete in WWE, but Kerry's father and four of his five brothers were all Superstars in the family business, WCCW. In 2009, the Von Erich family were inducted as a group into the WWE Hall of Fame.

SUPER STATS

HEIGHT: 6ft 2in (1.87m)

WEIGHT: 254lbs (115.21kg)

HOMETOWN: Dallas, Texas

SIGNATURE MOVE: Tornado Punch—Von Erich spins in a circle and punches his opponent.

MAIN RIVALS: Mr. Perfect, Ric Flair

KEVIN NASH

Almost seven-foot-tall stature makes Nash a WWE giant

HE ROSE TO THE TOP of WWE by becoming WWE Champion in 1995, but Kevin Nash's biggest impact would come after he left WWE in 1996 and joined WCW as one of the founding members of the nWo faction. The former "Big Daddy" used his size advantage and devastating Jackknife Powerbomb move to defeat many of the WCW Superstars, becoming a five-time WCW World Heavyweight Champion and nine-time WCW Tag Team Champion.

THE OUTSIDERS

In 1996, Nash invaded WCW with Scott Hall as the tag team the Outsiders. The duo pounced on announcer, Tony Schiavone, and commentator, Larry Zbyszko, and implied that they had been sent to WCW by WWE. They were actually part of the villainous nWo stable and were set on taking over all of sports entertainment.

SUPER STATS

HEIGHT: 6ft 10in (2.08m)

WEIGHT: 328lbs (148.77kg)

HOMETOWN: Detroit, Michigan

SIGNATURE MOVE: Jackknife Powerbomb—Nash picks up his opponent, lifts them up to the height of his head and shoulders, and drops them.

MAIN RIVALS: Big Show, Undertaker

KEVIN OWENS

THIS TRASH-TALKING Superstar from Quebec has built an impressive résumé in WWE within just a couple of years. With a sour attitude and a huge chip on his shoulder, Owens is a master of hurling both insults and fists—and he has no problem betraying his friends, including Chris Jericho or Sami Zayn, to get what he wants. The self-proclaimed "New Face of America" is a former NXT, United States, and WWE Universal Champion.

Initials decorated with the American flag to celebrate Owens winning the United States Championship

BEST ENEMIES FOREVER

Kevin Owens and Sami Zayn grew up together in Quebec. Best friends, they trained together for NXT and WWE—then their friendship soured when Owens jealously attacked Zayn after Zayn won the NXT Championship. Since then they have fought bitterly in intense matches.

SUPER STATS

HEIGHT: 6ft (1.82m)

WEIGHT: 266lbs (120.65kg)

HOMETOWN: Marieville, Quebec, Canada

SIGNATURE MOVE: Pop-up Powerbomb—Owens bounces his opponent off the ropes, throws them up in the air, and slams them down on their back.

MAIN RIVALS: John Cena, Sami Zayn

KONA REEVES

A FUN-LOVING, up-and-coming Superstar from Hawaii, Kona Reeves has been learning the ropes and growing his skills and techniques in NXT since 2013. Initially trained by WWE Hall of Famer Afa, of the Wild Samoans, Reeves continues to master his abilities by working out at the WWE Performance Center with head coach Albert and touring the world as part of the NXT brand.

Colorful Hawaiian shirt

SURF'S UP

In a shocking moment, Kona Reeves briefly got the upper hand in a match with No Way Jose by riding his opponents back like a surfboard! However, Jose came back and won the match a few minutes later.

SUPER STATS

HEIGHT: 6ft 3in (1.90m)

WEIGHT: 225lbs (102kg)

HOMETOWN: Orlando, Florida

SIGNATURE MOVE: Hawaiian drop—With his opponent on his shoulders, Reeves drops backward, driving his chest into the mat.

MAIN RIVALS: Hideo Itami, Aleister Black

KURT ANGLE

IT'S ONE THING to win an Olympic gold medal in freestyle wrestling; it's another to do so with a broken neck—but that's exactly what Kurt Angle did. Living his life by the "Three I's," (Intensity, Integrity, and Intelligence), the Olympic wrestling champion came to WWE and dominated the competition by winning almost every championship WWE had. His perfected technical skills earned him a spot in the WWE Hall of Fame in 2017.

Smart business suits are Kurt Angle's signature style

BUSINESS TIES

Kurt Angle was chosen to be the General Manager of *RAW* in April 2017. The position gives him the power to create matches and control the destinies of *RAW* Superstars such as Finn Bálor.

SUPER STATS

HEIGHT: 6ft (1.82m)

WEIGHT: 220lbs (99.79kg)

HOMETOWN: Pittsburgh, Pennsylvania

SIGNATURE MOVE: Angle Slam —Angle lifts his opponent onto his shoulders and tips backward, driving him onto the mat.

MAIN RIVALS: Brock Lesnar, Eddie Guerrero

LANA

Hair is always down for in-ring competition and up for managerial duties

DESCENDING FROM a wealthy Russian family, Lana is fiercely proud of her heritage. As a manager, "The Ravishing Russian" led her charges to victory through tactical analysis of their opponents and developing a winning strategy in the ring. Her passion for winning drove her to leave her managerial duties behind and enter the ring as a Superstar on *SmackDown Live*, where she has competed for the SmackDown Women's Championship.

THE PERFECT TEAM

What began as a manager-Superstar relationship blossomed into romance. Lana and Rusev walked into the ring together for years before walking down the wedding aisle in 2016. Despite being united in matrimony, when they're in the ring, it's all about business.

SUPER STATS

HEIGHT: 5ft 7in (1.70m)

HOMETOWN: Moscow, Russia

SIGNATURE MOVE: Sitout Spine Buster—Lana scoops up her opponent, turns them upside down, then slams them down on their back.

MAIN RIVALS: Brie Bella, Natalya

LEX LUGER

DID YOU KNOW?
Luger was a member of the nWo Wolfpac faction during his time in WCW.

NEVER FEARING A FIGHT, former member of The Four Horsemen and WCW Champion Lex Luger had to prove himself in WWE. Focusing on foes such as Yokozuna, Luger battled for the WWE Championship at *WrestleMania X*. Luger returned to WCW in a tag team with British Bulldog, shocking fans by appearing on the first episode of *WCW Monday Nitro* just one night after his final match for WWE.

Tough neck and shoulders assist with his Torture Rack maneuver

A metal plate in Luger's forearm, put in after a bike accident, made him even tougher

THE LEX EXPRESS

Lex Luger was victorious in a showdown with the near-600-pound WWE Champion Yokozuna on the deck of USS *Intrepid* aircraft carrier on America's Independence Day, July 4, 1993. Following his win, Luger promoted his patriotic message around the country on a bus called "The Lex Express."

SUPER STATS

HEIGHT: 6ft 6in (1.98m)

WEIGHT: 275lbs (124.73kg)

HOMETOWN: Chicago, Illinois

SIGNATURE MOVE: Torture Rack —Luger carries his opponent on his shoulders, stretching them by their neck and legs.

MAIN RIVALS: Yokozuna, Sting

LINCE DORADO

HE'S AS AGILE AS A cat, but Superstar Lince Dorado has claws, too, alongside a vicious streak in the ring. Dorado's name translates to "The Golden Lynx," and he is certainly a flashy competitor. He earned his wings in Japan and Mexico, then came to WWE to join the Cruiserweight Classic tournament. Dorado is now an important part of his division on *RAW* and *205 Live*.

Ring gear and mask based on a wild cat

Dorado's flashy look sets him apart as he claws his way to the top

TOP TIPS

Dorado trained for competition with WWE Superstars Cesaro and Kassius Ohno. They enhanced his high-flying antics by adding grounded moves to make him even more formidable.

SUPER STATS

HEIGHT: 5ft 7in (1.70m)

WEIGHT: 170lbs (77.11kg)

HOMETOWN: San Juan, Puerto Rico

SIGNATURE MOVE: Lynxsault —Dorado jumps off the rope and flips backward, landing on top of his opponent.

MAIN RIVALS: Rich Swann, Tony Nese

LITA

THIS LEGEND ONLY needs one name: Lita. First part of Team Xtreme with The Hardy Boyz, Lita loved high-flying action and fierce competition. With rival Trish Stratus, she tore the house down in countless battles over the Women's Championship. They were the first women to compete in the main event on *RAW*. Lita helped Edge pursue the WWE Title before retiring in 2006, and took her rightful place in the WWE Hall of Fame in 2014.

A NEW TITLE

At *WrestleMania 32*, Lita introduced a new title: the WWE Women's Championship. This crowning prize helped to recognize the extremely high level of talent among so many female competitors in sports entertainment.

SUPER STATS

HEIGHT: 5ft 6in (1.67m)

HOMETOWN: Sanford, North Carolina

SIGNATURE MOVE: Litacanrana —Lita grabs her opponent with her legs and flips her down.

MAIN RIVALS: Trish Stratus, Mickie James

LIV MORGAN

PROUDLY REPRESENTING

New Jersey, Liv Morgan will never back down from a challenge—and she's had her fair share of challenges competing in NXT's women's division. With her hi-tops, baseball caps and trademark acrobatic moves, Morgan shows off her fierce fighting spirit in every battle she takes on.

Cap displays Morgan's motto "Ya Only Liv Once"

AUSSIE ISSUES

Morgan has had many issues with the Australian duo of Billie Kay and Peyton Royce. But she has the skills to put them down under, defeating Kay and Royce in both tag team and singles matches.

SUPER STATS

HEIGHT: 5ft 3in (1.60m)

HOMETOWN: Elmwood Park, New Jersey

SIGNATURE MOVE: Reverse Roundhouse Kick—Morgan swings her leg behind her opponent's upper back in a stiff kick.

MAIN RIVALS: Billie Kay, Peyton Royce

LUKE HARPER

A MYSTERIOUS MOUNTAIN of a man, Luke Harper doesn't talk much, but his ruthless moves tell the story instead. He is fully focused on the win. A former member of the legendary (and very menacing) Wyatt Family, Harper has left the nest and is flying free in WWE. His opponents had better beware —this burly brawler crosses a ring quicker than expected for someone of his formidable size, and his strength is undeniable.

Sleeve protects Harper's arm as he delivers his Clothesline move

FAMILY BREAKUP

Harper was a longtime member of Bray Wyatt's "family," but after Wyatt took his rival Randy Orton on board, Harper knew it was time to leave. He turned on Wyatt and separated from his family.

SUPER STATS

HEIGHT: 6ft 5in (1.95m)

WEIGHT: 275lbs (124.73kg)

HOMETOWN: Rochester, New York

SIGNATURE MOVE: Discus Clothesline—Harper spins in a circle, blasting his opponent with an extended arm.

MAIN RIVALS: Erik Rowan, Dean Ambrose

"MACHO MAN" RANDY SAVAGE

Colorful cowboy hat tops glitzy ring gear

WITH HIS FAMOUS CATCHPHRASE "OOOH YEAH!," "Macho Man" Randy Savage became one of the most iconic Superstars in WWE. His personal intensity and flamboyance got him noticed, but his in-ring abilities made him a multi-time WCW and WWE World Champion. At *WrestleMania III*, Savage beat Ricky Steamboat in a show-stealing match that has been described as the greatest of all time. Savage joined the Hall of Fame in 2015.

DID YOU KNOW?

At *WrestleMania IV* in 1988, Savage battled and won a 14-man tournament to be crowned WWE Champion.

MACHO'S MATCH

For years, "The First Lady of WWE" and Savage's manager, Miss Elizabeth, walked him to the ring. They traded wedding rings at *SummerSlam 1991* in a ceremony dubbed "The Match Made in Heaven."

SUPER STATS

HEIGHT: 6ft 2in (1.87m)

WEIGHT: 237lbs (107.50kg)

HOMETOWN: Sarasota, Florida

SIGNATURE MOVE: Flying Elbow Drop—Savage dives off the top rope, landing his elbow on his opponent.

MAIN RIVALS: Diamond Dallas Page, Ultimate Warrior

MARK HENRY

DID YOU KNOW?

Early in his WWE career, Henry joined The Rock, Godfather, D-Lo Brown, and Ron Simmons in the Nation of Domination faction.

Ring gear inspired by Olympic weightlifting outfits

A HALL OF FAME induction is every Superstar's greatest dream, but joining Mark Henry's "Hall of Pain"? That's a complete nightmare. Claiming to be "The World's Strongest Man," Henry competed in weightlifting in the 1992 and 1996 Olympic Games. He uses his massive size and incredible strength to vanquish his opponents in the ring.

POWERSLAM

At *WWE Night of Champions 2011*, Henry faced Randy Orton for the World Heavyweight Championship. Orton hit Henry with his signature move, the RKO, but Henry hoisted Orton up and slammed him onto the mat, winning the title.

SUPER STATS

HEIGHT: 6ft 4in (1.93m)

WEIGHT: 360lbs (163.29kg)

HOMETOWN: Silsbee, Texas

SIGNATURE MOVE: World's Strongest Slam—Henry holds his opponent across his chest and drops to the ground crushing them under his massive frame.

MAIN RIVALS: Big Show, Shawn Michaels

MICHAEL HAYES

HE ROCKS THE CROWD even before he enters the ring. Fun-loving Superstar Michael Hayes is credited with being the first competitor to make his appearance with a signature rock tune. He made his name in Texas, competing in a heated rivalry against the Von Erich family. A multi-time tag team champion, Hayes was inducted into the WWE Hall of Fame in 2016.

WWE Hall of Fame ring, worn proudly

FREEBIRDS!

Hayes, Buddy Roberts, and Terry Gordy were the Fabulous Freebirds, a three-member tag team who won several championships in their 15 years together. Any two of the team could fight to defend a title.

SUPER STATS

HEIGHT: 6ft 4in (1.93m)

WEIGHT: 255lbs (115.66kg)

HOMETOWN: Atlanta, Georgia

SIGNATURE MOVE: DDT— Hayes holds his opponent bent over, facedown and drops them onto the mat.

MAIN RIVALS: Von Erich Family

125

MICK FOLEY

AS A TEENAGER, Mick Foley hitched rides to Madison Square Garden to attend WWE events, dreaming he would be in the ring one day. Mrs. Foley's Baby Boy began his quest in tiny venues around the world and soon found fans with his death-defying style. Foley has done it all—from winning world championships to becoming *RAW* General Manager and entering the WWE Hall of Fame in 2013.

Flannel suit for Foley's role as *RAW* General Manager

MANY FACES

The masked (and maybe dangerous) Mankind is one of three extreme personas Foley used during his in-ring career. The others were the unhinged Superstar Cactus Jack and the handsome hippy Dude Love.

SUPER STATS

HEIGHT: 6ft 2in (1.87m)

WEIGHT: 287lbs (130.18kg)

HOMETOWN: Long Island, New York

SIGNATURE MOVE: Mandible Claw—Foley grabs his opponent by the mouth and holds on tightly until they submit.

MAIN RIVALS: Undertaker, Vader

MICKIE JAMES

DID YOU KNOW?

Prior to her full-time return to WWE, James challenged NXT Women's Champion Asuka at *NXT Takeover: Toronto* in November 2016.

HER EYES ALWAYS on the prize, Mickie James debuted in WWE in 2005 and made an instant impact by defeating Trish Stratus for the WWE Women's Championship at *WrestleMania 22*. Five years and five women's championships later, James left WWE, but returned in 2017 to use her athletic skills and match-tested talent in pursuit of the *RAW* and *SmackDown* Women's Championships.

LA LUCHADORA

James returned to WWE disguised in a red mask and calling herself "La Luchadora." She helped then-SmackDown Women's Champion Alexa Bliss defeat Becky Lynch in a Cage Match. After Bliss's victory, James revealed herself.

SUPER STATS

HEIGHT: 5ft 4in (1.62m)

HOMETOWN: Richmond, Virginia

SIGNATURE MOVE: Mick Kick —James kicks her opponent high on their body.

MAIN RIVALS: Trish Stratus, Becky Lynch

MIKE AND MARIA KANELLIS

THE WWE UNIVERSE was introduced to the meaning of true love in June 2017 when Maria Kanellis returned to WWE at *Money in the Bank* alongside her husband, Mike. Maria had been a part of WWE since 2004 as a competitor and backstage interviewer, but she left the company in 2010 to find her "perfect partner." On arrival in WWE in 2017 the couple explained their plans to educate other *SmackDown Live* Superstars about the power of love.

DID YOU KNOW?

Maria Kanellis won the Slammy Award for "Diva of the Year." in 2009

Tattoo details the extent of Maria's love

PAST LIVES

For weeks, Sami Zayn kept interrupting Mike and Maria's show of love for each other. The couple were mad about this and challenged Sami to a match. But when Sami was about to attack Mike, Maria jumped in to protect her husband.

SUPER STATS

NAMES: Maria, Mike

HOMETOWN: Chicago, Illinois

SIGNATURE MOVE: Power of Love—Mike lifts his opponent on his shoulders and slams them down to the mat.

MAIN RIVAL: Sami Zayn

"EVERYBODY HAS A PRICE for the Million Dollar Man!" This was the bold claim "Million Dollar Man" Ted DiBiase backed up by paying off his opponents if he wasn't able to win by his own skill. When he learned he couldn't buy his way into owning the WWE Championship, DiBiase made his very own gold and diamond encrusted "Million Dollar Championship" Title to carry around with him.

Million Dollar Championship Title

MONEY MATTERS

After defeating his opponents, "Million Dollar Man" Ted DiBiase would shove a $100 note into their mouth, with his bodyguard, Virgil, ready to assist if necessary.

Always dressed to impress

SUPER STATS

HEIGHT: 6ft 1in (1.85m)

WEIGHT: 260lbs (118kg)

HOMETOWN: Palm Beach, Florida

SIGNATURE MOVE: Million Dollar Dream—DiBiase wraps his arms around his opponent's head and holds tight.

MAIN RIVALS: Dusty Rhodes, Jake "The Snake" Roberts

THE MIZ (WITH MARYSE)

A BONAFIDE MOVIE and reality television star, The Miz is a must-see competitor—and not only in WWE. When he's not competing, he's walking the red carpet at movie premieres or shooting his latest film. His Hollywood success has given him a big ego and provoked the ire of the WWE Universe. But as a former WWE Champion and seven-time Intercontinental Champion, The Miz has shown he is very much a Superstar.

DID YOU KNOW?

The Miz came in second place in the 4th season of WWE's *Tough Enough* TV series, earning him a WWE contract for his efforts.

Jacket is a Hollywood-inspired design

POWER COUPLE

The Miz is married to former WWE Divas Champion, Maryse. Together, they are one of WWE's most powerful couples, using their success in and out of the ring to demand better matches, nicer dressing rooms, and more attention.

SUPER STATS

HEIGHT: 6ft 2in (1.87m)

WEIGHT: 221lbs (100.24kg)

HOMETOWN: Hollywood, California

SIGNATURE MOVE: Skull-Crushing Finale—The Miz grabs his opponent and slams them down to the mat.

MAIN RIVALS: John Cena, Dean Ambrose

MOJO RAWLEY

THIS WWE SUPERSTAR has energy to spare. Mojo Rawley lives by his motto, "I don't get hyped, I stay hyped." The former professional football player came to WWE via NXT in 2013. After three years refining his in-ring skills, Rawley was drafted to *SmackDown Live* in 2016. Months later, Rawley won the André the Giant Memorial Battle Royal match at *WrestleMania 33*.

Rawley's ring gear ties lace up the front, similar to football uniform pants

THE HYPE BROS

During his time in NXT, Rawley formed a tag team called The Hype Bros with Zack Ryder. The dynamic duo later moved on to *SmackDown Live* where they conquered teams such as The Ascension. Go, Bros!

SUPER STATS

HEIGHT: 6ft 4in (1.93m)

WEIGHT: 265lbs (120kg)

HOMETOWN: Alexandria, Virginia

SIGNATURE MOVE: Hyperdrive —Rawley jumps high in the air and lands sitting on his opponent.

MAIN RIVALS: Wesley Blake and Buddy Murphy, Breezango

MR. PERFECT

PROVING JUST HOW "perfect" he could be, Mr. Perfect showed off his athletic ability to the WWE Universe by catching a field-length football pass he'd thrown to himself, nailing a blind full-court basketball shot, and knocking baseballs out of the park. His skills led to United States and Intercontinental Championships and a WWE Hall of Fame induction in 2007. Perfect.

"Absolutely perfect" physique, according to the man himself

DISROBED

Following his time in WWE, Hennig was made an honorary member of The Four Horsemen. But Mr. Perfect betrayed them, attacking leader Ric Flair at *Fall Brawl 1997*, stealing his robe, and handing it over to rivals.

SUPER STATS

HEIGHT: 6ft 3in (1.90m)

WEIGHT: 257lbs (116.57kg)

HOMETOWN: Robbinsdale, Minnesota

SIGNATURE MOVE: Perfect-Plex —Mr. Perfect hooks his opponent by the leg and arm, and flips them over his head into a pin.

MAIN RIVALS: Bret "Hit Man" Hart, Ric Flair

"MR. WONDERFUL" PAUL ORNDORFF

ICON, SUPERSTAR, and all-around "Mr. Wonderful", Paul Orndorff competed in memorable WWE events in the 1980s. He battled in a Steel Cage Match on one of the first episodes of *Saturday Night's Main Event,* and challenged the legendary Superstar Tony Atlas at "The War to Settle the Score," an event that aired on MTV. Orndorff was a wonderful addition to the WWE Hall of Fame in 2005.

DID YOU KNOW?

After his retirement in 1995, Orndorff coached at WCW's Power Plant where he trained future WWE Universal Champion Goldberg.

Strong upper body for performing piledrivers

TRASH-TALKERS

Orndorff and "Rowdy" Roddy Piper often brought chaos to WWE with their trash talking. The pair were challenged to a tag team match against Hulk Hogan and Mr. T in the main event of the first *WrestleMania.*

SUPER STATS

HEIGHT: 6ft (1.82m)

WEIGHT: 252lbs (114.30kg)

HOMETOWN: Brandon, Florida

SIGNATURE MOVE: Piledriver— Orndorff holds his opponent upside down and sits down, dropping them to the mat.

MAIN RIVALS: "Rowdy" Roddy Piper, "Cowboy" Bob Orton

MUSTAFA ALI

DID YOU KNOW?
Before his career in sports entertainment, Mustafa Ali was a police officer in Chicago.

Colors of Pakistani flag honor Ali's roots

HIGH-FLYING SUPERSTAR

Mustafa Ali made his WWE debut in 2016. Like many in the cruiserweight division, Ali joined WWE after sharpening his skills in the Cruiserweight Classic tournament. Ali uses his arsenal of dramatic aerial moves in his matches on *RAW* and *205 Live*, much to the chagrin of his chief rival, Drew Gulak, who is against using high-flying moves.

CRUISIN'

In 2016, WWE created a new category for its Superstars: the cruiserweight division. To be eligible, Superstars must weigh less than 205 pounds (92.98 kilos). Ali's weight helps him perform high-flying kicks against opponents such as TJP.

SUPER STATS

HEIGHT: 5ft 10in (1.77m)

WEIGHT: 182lbs (82.50kg)

HOMETOWN: Chicago, Illinois

SIGNATURE MOVE: Inverted 450 Splash—while his opponent lies on the mat, Ali jumps backward and flips down onto them.

MAIN RIVALS: Drew Gulak, Lince Dorado

NAOMI

BEGINNING HER CAREER in WWE as a dancer, Naomi transitioned to being a WWE Superstar and went in full pursuit of championships in the *SmackDown Live* Women's Division. Naomi faces her opponents fearlessly with an in-ring style that combines athleticism and artistic flair. With these outstanding skills at her disposal, Naomi has pledged that each and every WWE Superstar will "Feel the Glow" and fall to defeat at her hands.

Neon designs glow during Naomi's ring entrance

Bright hair color glows in the dark

LIVING THE DREAM

Naomi dreamed of winning the WWE Women's Championship, and worked hard to do so. After defeating Alexa Bliss for the Title at 2017's *Elimination Chamber* event, Naomi held the Title high and was greeted by chants of "you deserve it!" from the WWE Universe.

SUPER STATS

HEIGHT: 5ft 5in (1.65m)

HOMETOWN: Orlando, Florida

SIGNATURE MOVE: Slay-O-Mission—Naomi wraps her legs around her opponent's shoulders and applies pressure to force them to submit.

MAIN RIVALS: Alexa Bliss, Charlotte Flair

NASTY BOYS

DID YOU KNOW?

The Nasty Boys defeated Bret "Hit Man" Hart and Jim "The Anvil" Neidhart to win their first-ever WWE Tag Team Championship.

MESSY, ILL-MANNERED, and all around gross, the Nasty Boys were a quirky addition to the WWE tag team division. Their general nastiness was combined with a ruthlessness that led them to obtain tag team championship gold at *WrestleMania VII*. Unafraid of fighting dirty, the Nasty Boys often used whatever they could find around the ring to subdue their opponents.

Tooth lost in one of the Nasty Boys' vicious brawls

THE MOUTH OF THE SOUTH

The Nasty Boys were managed by Jimmy Hart, who called himself "The Mouth of the South." Hart was known for screaming instructions to his Superstars from the ringside using a bullhorn to enhance his voice.

SUPER STATS

NAMES: Jerry Sags, Brian Knobbs

WEIGHT: 546lbs (247.66kg)

HOMETOWN: Nastyville

SIGNATURE MOVE: Pit Stop —Knobbs shoves their opponent's face into Sags raised armpit.

MAIN RIVALS: Natural Disasters, The Hart Foundation

NATALYA

DID YOU KNOW?

Natalya has a big heart outside of the ring and gives her time to several charities.

Pink and black colors of the Hart family

THE FIRST FEMALE third-generation WWE Superstar, Natalya has sports entertainment in her DNA. As a member of the legendary Hart Family, she was raised in the ring. Like her father, Jim "The Anvil" Neidhart, and uncles Bret "Hit Man" Hart and the British Bulldog, Natalya uses a mix of powerhouse strikes and technical submission moves in the ring. She refers to herself as the "Queen of Harts," and hopes to add the Women's Championship to her family's golden legacy.

STU'S DUNGEON

Natalya trained in her grandfather, Stu Hart's basement, known as the Dungeon. Stu, a WWE Hall of Famer, taught countless Superstars how to compete there, and made himself a legendary part of WWE history.

SUPER STATS

HEIGHT: 5ft 5in (1.65m)

HOMETOWN: Calgary, Alberta, Canada

SIGNATURE MOVE: Sharpshooter —Natalya twists her opponent's legs around hers and leans back.

MAIN RIVALS: Nikki Bella, Becky Lynch

NATURAL DISASTERS

HERE COMES TROUBLE: half a ton of it. The Natural Disasters—Earthquake and Typhoon—were as devastating as their name implied. Their massive frames caused tremors in the ring. The gigantic Superstars let loose their wrath on the other tag teams in WWE. Their greatest achievement was winning the Tag Team championship in 1992.

Ring gear features the Richter scale, used to measure quake tremors

TUGBOAT

Prior to joining forces with Earthquake, Typhoon competed in singles action under the name Tugboat. Dressed in a sailor hat and jaunty stripes, Tugboat earned the love of the WWE Universe, who echoed his tugboat-horn call as he walked to the ring.

SUPER STATS

NAMES: Fred "Typhoon" Ottman, John "Earthquake" Tenta

COMBINED WEIGHT: 846lbs (383.73kg)

SIGNATURE MOVE: Splash—Earthquake and Typhoon jump and land on their opponent either on the mat or in the ring corner.

MAIN RIVALS: The Nasty Boys, Money, Inc.

NEVILLE

THE MAN THAT gravity forgot, Neville launched his career with NXT where he won and held the NXT Championship for 287 days in 2014. Now, the ambitious Superstar is flying high in WWE's cruiserweight division. Neville captured the Cruiserweight Championship by defeating Rich Swann at the 2017 *Royal Rumble*. Since then, he has dominated his division, declaring himself "King of the Cruiserweights."

Gauntlets protect Neville's wrists from injury

RULING ARIES

To retain his cruiserweight crown, Neville had to fend off challenges from Austin Aries. Their most vicious bout was at *WrestleMania 33*, with Neville reigning supreme.

SUPER STATS

HEIGHT: 5ft 8in (1.72m)

WEIGHT: 194lbs (88kg)

HOMETOWN: Newcastle, UK

SIGNATURE MOVE: Red Arrow —Neville dives off the top rope, twisting and flipping in the air, and lands on his opponent.

MAIN RIVALS: Austin Aries, TJP

NEW AGE OUTLAWS

"OH, YOU DIDN'T KNOW?" was a phrase that ignited the crowd when it was called out by Brian James during matches. As members of the chaos-causing D-Generation X faction, New Age Outlaws were rebellious at every opportunity and didn't care about following the rules or respecting their opponents. They used their unruly ways to become six-time WWE Tag Team Champions.

Billy Gunn wears the team colors—green and black

Making an "X"—the sign of D-Generation X

INVASION

The New Age Outlaws, dressed in camo and joined by Triple H and X-Pac, drove an armored military vehicle to invade a live broadcast of rival WCW's *Monday Nitro*.

SUPER STATS

NAMES: Billy Gunn, "Road Dogg" Jesse James

COMBINED WEIGHT: 501lbs (227.25kg)

SIGNATURE MOVE: Spike Piledriver—Gunn holds their opponent upside down while James grabs their legs and pushes them down onto the mat.

MAIN RIVALS: Mick Foley and Terry Funk, The Shield

THE NEW DAY

DID YOU KNOW?
Xavier Woods's trombone, named Francesca is the tag team's beloved mascot.

PROPELLED TO GREATNESS

by the power of positivity, The New Day are one of the most popular tag teams in WWE history. Whether sharing their own brand of "Booty-O's" cereal with the WWE Universe or performing energetic moves in the ring, they always put smiles on people's faces. Plus, the trio have captured the WWE Tag Team Championship three times since their WWE debut in 2014.

Bright ring gear for an eye-catching entrance

LONGEST REIGN

In 2016 The New Day set a record for the longest-reigning Tag Team Champions—483 days. They crushed Seth Rollins and Roman Reigns, and Chris Jericho and his partner Kevin Owens, to win.

SUPER STATS

NAMES: Big E, Kofi Kingston, and Xavier Woods

COMBINED WEIGHT: 702lbs (318.42kg)

SIGNATURE MOVE: Midnight Hour—Woods or Kingston jump off the top rope, driving the opponent off Big E's shoulder and onto the mat.

MAIN RIVALS: Cesaro, Sheamus, The Usos

NIA JAX

DID YOU KNOW?

Jax is related to WWE Superstars The Rock, the Usos, and Roman Reigns.

Height puts Jax head and shoulders above rivals

INTIMIDATING ALL WHO stand against her, Nia Jax is a seemingly unstoppable force in the women's divisions of NXT and *RAW*. At 6 foot, Jax towers over the other female Superstars in WWE, and she is reaching for the top in the women's division, too. She uses her unmatched strength and agility to punish opponents. She has designs on winning the Women's Championship, and will destroy any Superstar who stands in her way.

Strong arms can squeeze the air from her opponents

BREAKING GROUND

Like many WWE Superstars, Jax trained at WWE's Performance Center, where she broke weight-lifting records. Jax's personal journey from the Performance Center to NXT and WWE featured in the WWE Network reality TV series "Breaking Ground."

SUPER STATS

HEIGHT: 6ft (1.82m)

HOMETOWN: San Diego, California

SIGNATURE MOVE: Leg Drop—Jax jumps and sits on her opponent on the mat.

MAIN RIVALS: Alexa Bliss, Bayley

NIKKI BELLA

HER MOTTO IS "Fearless" and Nikki Bella backs it up every time she enters the ring. Bella began her WWE career with her twin sister Brie, appearing alongside *RAW's* celebrity guest hosts. That wasn't enough for Nikki, who channeled her competitive nature into training for in-ring competition. She honed her athletic skills to compete in the ring, earning double WWE Divas Championships.

Cap features Bella Twin symbol

"Fearless" motto features on ring gear

DIVAS CHAMP

Bella powered her way to victory over AJ Lee to win her second Divas Championship at the 2014 *Survivor Series*. She would go on to hold the title for a record-setting 301 days.

SUPER STATS

HEIGHT: 5ft 6in (1.67m)

HOMETOWN: San Diego, California

SIGNATURE MOVE: Rack Attack 2.0—Bella lifts her opponent on her shoulders, and throws her behind her as she jumps down.

MAIN RIVALS: Natalya, Carmella

NOAM DAR

"THE SCOTTISH SUPERNOVA,"

Noam Dar represented both his Israeli birthplace and his Scottish home in the WWE Cruiserweight Classic tournament in 2016. Dar battled all the way to the quarterfinals before being eliminated by Zack Sabre, Jr. He is a mat-focused competitor, preferring submission holds to high-risk aerial maneuvers.

Flashy ring gear defies in-ring style

Space theme perfect for a "Supernova"

ARCH RIVALS

Dar's fiercest rival in WWE has been Cedric Alexander. The two cruiserweight Superstars also fought over the affections of Alicia Fox, who joined Dar's side after he defeated Alexander on *205 Live*.

SUPER STATS

HEIGHT: 5ft 9in (1.75m)

WEIGHT: 178lbs (80.73kg)

HOMETOWN: Ayr, Scotland

SIGNATURE MOVE: Kneebar— Dar wraps his opponent's knee over his own, and bends it in a painful submission move.

MAIN RIVAL: Cedric Alexander

NO WAY JOSE

DANCING HIS WAY to the ring, No Way Jose always brings excitement and energy to a match. The Superstar loves to get down, but he's certainly no walkover. He will defend himself vigorously, hitting as hard as he is light on this feet. As soon as any hard-fought match is over, however, No Way Jose goes right back to dancing the night away.

Logo tells the WWE Universe the party never stops with No Way Jose

DANCING MACHINES

Jose joined forces with fellow dance-loving Superstar Rich Swann to battle in the 2016 Dusty Rhodes Tag Team Invitational. The dancing duo won their first round match, defeating Tony Nese and Drew Gulak.

SUPER STATS

HEIGHT: 6ft 3in (1.90m)

WEIGHT: 245lbs (111.13kg)

HOMETOWN: Santo Domingo, Dominican Republic

SIGNATURE MOVE: The Pitch—Jose lifts his opponent up by his shoulders, and slams him to the mat.

MAIN RIVALS: Austin Aries, Eric Young

ONEY LORCAN

HE'LL HIT YOU, stretch you, and ruthlessly defeat you. For Oney Lorcan, it's just another day on the mat. Lorcan plies his craft primarily in NXT, but has also battled the cruiserweights of *205 Live*. Tough as nails, Lorcan learned his fighting style on the streets of Boston. He claims to feel no pain, and has proven it by powering through brutal injuries to win matches. He is here for one purpose: to punish.

Stern expression for a no-nonsense brawler

POWER PUNCH

Oney brings his game right off the street and he puts all his might behind every move. He delivered his hard-and-fast message with a bare-knuckled punch that sent Tye Dillinger flying.

Old-school ring gear matches Orney's classic tactics

SUPER STATS

HEIGHT: 6ft 1in (1.85m)

WEIGHT: 190lbs (86kg)

HOMETOWN: Boston, Massachusetts

SIGNATURE MOVE: Single Leg Boston Crab—Lorcan turns his opponent on their stomach on the mat and pulls back hard on one of their legs, causing a submission.

MAIN RIVALS: Drew McIntyre, Hideo Itami

PAIGE

SHE SAYS WWE is her house, and Paige shows why every time she steps into the ring. Paige's family held sports entertainment events in their home town, and Paige learned how to compete in the ring from the time she was a small child. Dominating the women's division in NXT, Paige was the first NXT Women's Champion. She won The Divas Championship on her first night in WWE—the night after *WrestleMania 30* in 2014.

Paige is known for the shrieking scream that she lets out before matches

Paige's dark gear reflects her self-given nickname, "The Anti-Diva"

TEAM PCB

Paige needed backup against her enemies, The Bella Twins, so she teamed up with Charlotte Flair and Becky Lynch as part of WWE's Women's Revolution becoming Team PCB.

SUPER STATS

HEIGHT: 5ft 8in (1.72m)

HOMETOWN: Norwich, England

SIGNATURE MOVE: Paige Turner—Paige grabs her opponent by the arm and leg and spins them backward to the mat.

MAIN RIVALS: Charlotte Flair, Natalya

PEYTON ROYCE

BALLERINAS TWIRL, but Peyton Royce uses her dance skills and the athleticism of an NXT Superstar to twist her opponents into knots. Raised in Australia, Royce moved to Canada to train with WWE legend Lance Storm. As part of "The Iconic Duo," alongside lifelong friend Billie Kay, Royce has defeated top NXT Superstars on her way up.

Royce's mental focus shows in her expression

DEFEATING LIV

Royce has a great dislike for NXT Superstar Liv Morgan. After sneak-attacking Morgan repeatedly, Royce also faced her in several matches, and got her revenge by scoring pinfall and submission victories.

SUPER STATS

HEIGHT: 5ft 7in (1.70m)

HOMETOWN: Sydney, Australia

SIGNATURE MOVE: Fisherman Suplex—Royce grabs her opponent's arm and leg and flips them over her head to land in a pinning combination.

MAIN RIVALS: Liv Morgan, Asuka

RANDY ORTON

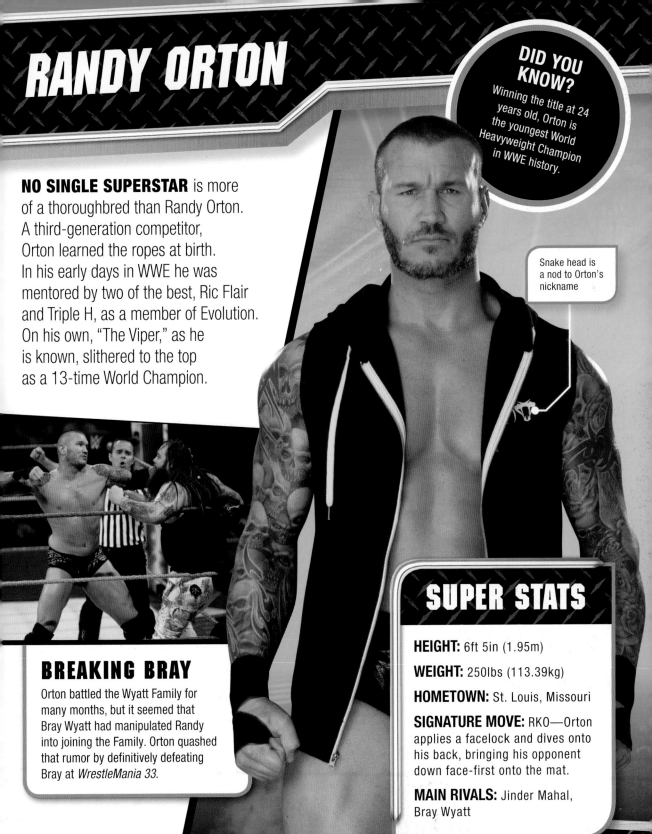

NO SINGLE SUPERSTAR is more of a thoroughbred than Randy Orton. A third-generation competitor, Orton learned the ropes at birth. In his early days in WWE he was mentored by two of the best, Ric Flair and Triple H, as a member of Evolution. On his own, "The Viper," as he is known, slithered to the top as a 13-time World Champion.

Snake head is a nod to Orton's nickname

BREAKING BRAY

Orton battled the Wyatt Family for many months, but it seemed that Bray Wyatt had manipulated Randy into joining the Family. Orton quashed that rumor by definitively defeating Bray at *WrestleMania 33*.

SUPER STATS

HEIGHT: 6ft 5in (1.95m)

WEIGHT: 250lbs (113.39kg)

HOMETOWN: St. Louis, Missouri

SIGNATURE MOVE: RKO—Orton applies a facelock and dives onto his back, bringing his opponent down face-first onto the mat.

MAIN RIVALS: Jinder Mahal, Bray Wyatt

"RAVISHING" RICK RUDE

Famous pre-match pose

ALL MOUTH and muscles, "Ravishing" Rick Rude insulted every member of the WWE Universe. Rude knew his physique was impressive, and he backed up his bragging with a show of sheer skill. The Intercontinental Champion was forced to retire early, but returned to WWE as a bodyguard for D-Generation X.

DID YOU KNOW?

"Ravishing" Rick Rude was inducted into the WWE Hall of Fame in 2017.

Ring gear painted with opponent's face for matches

TOO RUDE

Rick Rude made sports entertainment history on November 17, 1997, when he appeared on both WWE's Monday Night *RAW* and WCW's *Monday Nitro* on the same night.

SUPER STATS

HEIGHT: 6ft 3in (1.90m)

WEIGHT: 252lbs (114.30kg)

HOMETOWN: Robbinsdale, Minnesota

SIGNATURE MOVE: Rude Awakening—Rude grabs his opponent back-to-back, and pulls them down to the mat.

MAIN RIVALS: Jake "The Snake" Roberts, Ultimate Warrior

THE REVIVAL

MANY SUPERSTARS like to show off their flashy moves, but The Revival are the exact opposite. Their motto is "No flips, just fists," and they live up to that in every match. Their hard-hitting style in the ring earned them the NXT Tag Team Championship on two occasions. Since joining *RAW*, The Revival has demonstrated their toughness against top tag teams such as The Hardy Boyz and Enzo and Cass.

Clenched fists for heavy hitters in the ring

Wilder's simple trunks reflect the Revival's emphasis on substance over style

ALPHA MALES

The Revival's greatest opponents in NXT were American Alpha. The Revival faced them many times, including at *NXT TakeOver: The End* where The Revival won the Tag Team Championship.

SUPER STATS

NAMES: Dash Wilder, Scott Dawson

COMBINED WEIGHT: 446lbs (202.30kg)

SIGNATURE MOVE: Shatter Machine—Dawson lifts their opponent skyward as Wilder pulls them downward, hitting them with his knees as he falls.

MAIN RIVALS: The New Day, #DIY, American Alpha

RHYNO

DID YOU KNOW?
In addition to winning the tag titles, Rhyno is a former United States and Hardcore Champion.

Beastly scowl strikes fear in the ring

BUILT LIKE THE ANIMAL

that shares his name, Rhyno is solid muscle. With his powerful Gore tackle, the Superstar known as "The Man Beast" runs riot in the ring. Returning to WWE in 2015 after a decade's hiatus, Rhyno formed a *SmackDown Live* Championship tag team with Heath Slater.

Being hit by Rhyno's Gore move is like being hit by a truck

EXTREME!

Rhyno competed in Extreme Championship Wrestling (ECW) until 2001, when WWE purchased the company. He was both ECW Champion and ECW Television Champion.

SUPER STATS

HEIGHT: 5ft 10in (1.77m)

WEIGHT: 295lbs (133.81kg)

HOMETOWN: Detroit, Michigan

SIGNATURE MOVE: Gore—Rhyno tackles his opponent around the waist, taking them to the mat.

MAIN RIVALS: Chris Jericho, Wyatt Family

RIC FLAIR

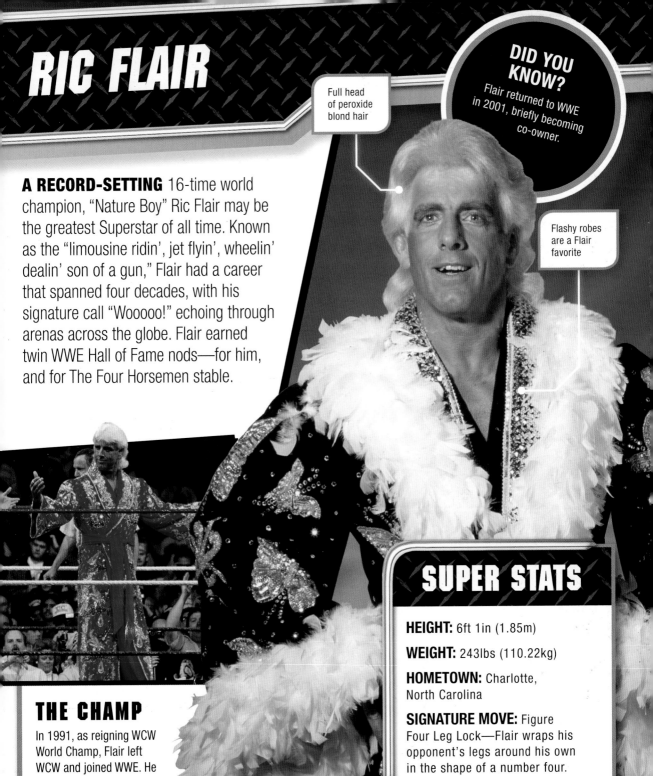

A RECORD-SETTING 16-time world champion, "Nature Boy" Ric Flair may be the greatest Superstar of all time. Known as the "limousine ridin', jet flyin', wheelin' dealin' son of a gun," Flair had a career that spanned four decades, with his signature call "Wooooo!" echoing through arenas across the globe. Flair earned twin WWE Hall of Fame nods—for him, and for The Four Horsemen stable.

Full head of peroxide blond hair

Flashy robes are a Flair favorite

THE CHAMP

In 1991, as reigning WCW World Champ, Flair left WCW and joined WWE. He then declared himself the "Real World's Champion" to the WWE Universe.

SUPER STATS

HEIGHT: 6ft 1in (1.85m)

WEIGHT: 243lbs (110.22kg)

HOMETOWN: Charlotte, North Carolina

SIGNATURE MOVE: Figure Four Leg Lock—Flair wraps his opponent's legs around his own in the shape of a number four.

MAIN RIVALS: Sting, Ricky "The Dragon" Steamboat

RICH SWANN

"CAN YOU HANDLE THIS?" With this question ringing in the ears of the WWE Universe, Rich Swann dances his way to the ring commanding the attention of the crowd *and* his opponents. Competing in both NXT and the WWE cruiserweight division, Swann snared the WWE Cruiserweight Championship from The Brian Kendrick on *205 Live*, letting everyone know he was the Superstar to watch.

Smile and charisma helps Swann gain the support of the WWE Universe

AIRBORNE

Like many of his cruiserweight cohorts, Swann uses flashy aerial maneuvers to defeat his opponents. Whether diving off the ropes or simply jumping high off the mat, Swann delights with his cool moves.

Wings for swan namesake and high-flying moves

SUPER STATS

HEIGHT: 5ft 8in (1.72m)

WEIGHT: 168lbs (76.20kg)

HOMETOWN: Baltimore, Maryland

SIGNATURE MOVE: Standing 450 Splash—Swann stands over his opponent as they lay on the mat, jumps in the air, and rotates 450 degrees to land on his opponent.

MAIN RIVALS: Neville, Noam Dar

RICKY STEAMBOAT

AS A NIMBLE SUPERSTAR, Ricky Steamboat won respect with his technical wizardry. Mixing high-flying attacks with martial arts, Steamboat captured the imaginations of the WWE Universe as well as the WWE Intercontinental and WCW World Heavyweight Championships. Steamboat was inducted into the WWE Hall of Fame into 2009 by his greatest rival, Ric Flair.

Headband features dragon scales

FIRED UP

Steamboat lived up to his nickname "The Dragon" in the 1990s. Clad in scales and wings, he literally breathed fire in the ring before his equally flamboyant matches.

SUPER STATS

HEIGHT: 5ft 10in (1.77m)

WEIGHT: 235lbs (106.60kg)

HOMETOWN: Honolulu, Hawaii

SIGNATURE MOVE: Diving Crossbody—Steamboat dives off the top rope, landing on top of his opponent at a right angle.

MAIN RIVALS: Ric Flair, "Macho Man" Randy Savage

RIKISHI

DID YOU KNOW?

Rikishi originally competed in WWE under the name Fatu before changing it to "Rikishi"—the Japanese word for sumo wrestler.

A SAMOAN GIANT known for his incredible agility, Rikishi used his massive body to squash his opposition in the ring. Rikishi drew on his training in the ancient Japanese art of sumo wrestling to win the Intercontinental and Tag Team Championships. Literally throwing his weight around, Rikishi terrified opponents with his "Stink Face" move, which involved sitting on the face of his opponents.

Shell necklace links Rikishi to his island heritage

SMOOTH MOVES

Rikishi loves hip-hop dance moves. He showed off his skills at many WWE events, including dancing at his 2015 WWE Hall of Fame induction alongside his Superstar sons, Jey and Jimmy Uso.

Traditional sumo belt named "mawashi"

SUPER STATS

HEIGHT: 6ft 1in (1.85m)

WEIGHT: 425lbs (192.77kg)

HOMETOWN: Samoa

SIGNATURE MOVE: Rikishi Driver —Rikishi picks up his opponent, places them on his shoulder and jump-sits down on the mat, driving down his opponent.

MAIN RIVALS: Edge, Stone Cold Steve Austin

ROB VAN DAM

ALWAYS RELAXED, Rob Van Dam takes life as it comes, and never gets upset about anything. He made his name in ECW and invaded WWE in 2001. With his martial arts skills and lightning-quick reflexes, "Mr. Monday Night," as he is known, won the European, Intercontinental, Tag Team, and Hardcore Titles, and cashed in the Money in the Bank suitcase to become a WWE Champion.

Yin and yang symbol highlights the martial arts

HARDCORE CHAMP

RVD won his first WWE Title, the Hardcore Championship, by beating Jeff Hardy at 2001's *Invasion* pay-per-view event. The Hardcore Title is defended in matches fought without rules for 24 hours a day, seven days a week.

SUPER STATS

HEIGHT: 6ft (1.82m)

WEIGHT: 235lbs (106.60kg)

HOMETOWN: Battle Creek, Michigan

SIGNATURE MOVE: Five Star Frog Splash—RVD leaps from the top rope, extending and retracting his limbs mid-air, and crashes onto his opponent.

MAIN RIVALS: John Cena, William Regal

THE ROCK

A THIRD GENERATION Superstar, The Rock has been an icon since his debut in 1996. A ten-time WWE World Heavyweight Champion, The Rock has headlined numerous *WrestleMania* events, beaten some of the best Superstars in WWE history, and defines WWE for millions of fans. He has become one of the biggest names in Hollywood, but he will forever be known as "the most electrifying man in sports entertainment."

Tattoo tells the story of The Rock's family and life in Samoan symbols

Bull tattoo refers to one of the Rock's nicknames, "The Brahma Bull"

THE ROCK SAYS...

The Rock is known for his many bold and cutting catchphrases, including: "If ya smell what The Rock is cookin'...", "Just bring it!", "It doesn't matter what you think!", and "Know your role and shut your mouth!"

SUPER STATS

HEIGHT: 6ft 5in (1.95m)

WEIGHT: 260lbs (118kg)

HOMETOWN: Miami, Florida

SIGNATURE MOVE: The People's Elbow—The Rock criss-crosses the ring before dropping his elbow onto his opponent.

MAIN RIVALS: John Cena, Stone Cold Steve Austin

ROCKY JOHNSON

TODAY BEST KNOWN as the father of The Rock, Rocky Johnson was a legendary Superstar in his own right. Trained by the man who would later become his father-in-law, High Chief Peter Maivia, Johnson competed against legends such as Harley Race and Terry Funk. He became the first African-American WWE Tag Team Champion in 1983 by defeating his cousins-in-law, the Wild Samoans.

Physique gained from training as a boxer

Twin tattoos of sparrows

HALL OF FAME
In 2008, Rocky Johnson received the greatest honor of his legendary career: admittance into the WWE Hall of Fame. The award was made even sweeter by being inducted by his son, The Rock.

SUPER STATS

HEIGHT: 6ft 2in (1.87m)

WEIGHT: 260lbs (118kg)

HOMETOWN: Toronto, Canada

SIGNATURE MOVE: Dropkick —Johnson leaps in the air, kicking his opponent with both feet.

MAIN RIVAL: The Wild Samoans

RODERICK STRONG

STRONG IS A SUPERSTAR with a purpose: to provide a better life for his son than he himself had as a child. Strong overcame a difficult childhood to find success in the ring. In his early years, he competed all over the world against next-generation Superstars such as Samoa Joe, Daniel Bryan, and Sami Zayn. Upon joining NXT, Strong battled SAnitY leader Eric Young, defeating him at *NXT Takeover Chicago* in 2017.

Strong's logo on his ring gear

TAG TEAMMATES

Longtime friend Austin Aries introduced Strong to WWE. The duo entered the second annual Dusty Rhodes Tag Team Classic tournament together and won their first match.

SUPER STATS

HEIGHT: 5ft 10in (1.77m)

WEIGHT: 200lbs (90.71kg)

HOMETOWN: Tampa, Florida

SIGNATURE MOVE: Sick Kick —Strong runs toward his opponent and hits them with a big kick in the chest.

MAIN RIVAL: SAnitY

ROMAN REIGNS

INTRODUCED TO WWE

as the powerful "Enforcer of The Shield", Roman Reigns is now known as "The Big Dog," and WWE is his yard. The former WWE Champion is a fierce competitor with incredible strength. He's used that strength to power through the best competitors in WWE, fighting his way to the top and becoming a three-time WWE Champion.

DID YOU KNOW?

Reigns defeated the legendary Undertaker, at *WrestleMania 33*, ending the Superstar's illustrious in-ring career.

Spike logo is a nod to Reigns's devastating Spear move

Fist clenched ready to unleash vicious Superman Punch move

DOG VS. BEAST

Reigns defeated 29 Superstars to win the Royal Rumble Match and earn a match against WWE Champion "The Beast" Brock Lesnar. The rivals met in an epic battle for the WWE Championship at *WrestleMania 31*.

SUPER STATS

HEIGHT: 6ft 3in (1.90m)

WEIGHT: 265lbs (120kg)

HOMETOWN: Pensacola, Florida

SIGNATURE MOVE: Spear—Reigns dives toward his opponent, tackling them to the mat.

MAIN RIVALS: Brock Lesnar, Braun Strowman

RON SIMMONS

JUST FIVE YEARS into his 20-year career, Ron Simmons made sports entertainment history when he became the first African-American World Heavyweight Champion by capturing the WCW Title from Lex Luger. Simmons led The Nation of Domination faction where he helped to mentor several Superstars-in-the-making. He later became a three-time WWE Tag Team Champion as a member of the APA tag team.

Crimson and gold, the colors of Florida State University

FAROOQ
When he first entered WWE, Simmons went by the name Farooq and dressed in a colorful gladiator-style costume.

SUPER STATS

HEIGHT: 6ft 2in (1.87m)

WEIGHT: 270lbs (122.47kg)

HOMETOWN: Warner Robins, Georgia

SIGNATURE MOVE: Dominator —Simmons lifts his opponent onto his shoulder, and flips them down onto the mat.

MAIN RIVALS: Lex Luger, The Rock

RODDY PIPER

ALWAYS CONTROVERSIAL, "Rowdy" Roddy Piper spoke his mind, made people angry, and fought with fury. Piper loved being unpredictable, always bragging, "Just when you think you have all the answers, I change the questions!" He won the Intercontinental Championship late in his career in 1992, and served for a short time as President of WWE during the late 1990s, where he organized matches and enforced the rules.

Piper's explosive personality earned him the nickname "Hot Rod"

PIPER'S PIT

From the 1980s through the 2000s, Piper hosted *Piper's Pit,* a wildly unpredictable talk show segment. Fights broke out, challenges were made, and guests such as S.D. Jones were insulted—all by Piper.

SUPER STATS

HEIGHT: 6ft 2in (1.87m)

WEIGHT: 230lbs (104.32kg)

HOMETOWN: Glasgow, Scotland

SIGNATURE MOVE: Sleeper Hold—Piper holds tight around the top of his opponent until they submit.

MAIN RIVALS: Goldust, Ric Flair

Kilt is traditional Scottish attire

RUBY RIOT

WITH A PUNK ROCKER attitude and a wild in-ring style, Ruby Riot came to NXT with two goals—to take down SAnitY member Nikki Cross and become NXT Women's Champion. Every time Riot and cross confront each other brutal brawls ensue, with neither Superstar having a clear advantage. Riot's efforts in obtaining the Women's Championship so far haven't been successful, but she continues to fight hard for it.

Chest and full sleeve tattoos

ANTI-SANITY

Riot's disdain for Nikki Cross has grown to include Cross's fellow SAnitY team members. Riot will attack any member of the dreaded faction—male or female—including Killian Dain at *NXT TakeOver: Orlando* in 2017.

Rockstar hand signs

SUPER STATS

HEIGHT: 5ft 4in (1.62m)

HOMETOWN: Lafayette, Indiana

SIGNATURE MOVE: Overhead Kick—Riot jumps and kicks at the top of her opponent's body.

MAIN RIVALS: Asuka, Nikki Cross

R-TRUTH

RAPPING HIS WAY to the ring, R-Truth asks the WWE Universe to echo his trademark call, "What's Up?" Debuting in WWE in 1999, R-Truth is a veteran Superstar who has captured attention with his unpredictable antics and with his suberb in-ring skill. He has racked up championships including the United States and Tag Team Titles.

Tattoo of initial and logo

LITTLE JIMMY

R-Truth's active imagination has led to many memorable moments, but nothing quite stood out like his reveal of "Little Jimmy," R-Truth's imaginary friend. R-Truth believed "Little Jimmy" helped him win matches, and insisted the referee also raise Jimmy's invisible hand in victory.

SUPER STATS

HEIGHT: 6ft 2in (1.87m)

WEIGHT: 220lbs (99.79kg)

HOMETOWN: Charlotte, North Carolina

SIGNATURE MOVE: Lie Detector —R-Truth jumps toward his opponent and spins in a corkscrew fashion, hitting them in the process.

MAIN RIVALS: Goldust, The Miz

RUSEV

"THE BULGARIAN BRUTE" Rusev exploded on the scene first in NXT and then in WWE, using his massive strength to crush his opposition. Rusev was undefeated in WWE competition from January 2014 through March 2015, winning the United States Championship along the way. The first Bulgarian-born WWE Superstar in history, Rusev is fiercely patriotic about his homeland.

Colors of his home country, Bulgaria

BRUTAL BATTLE

Rusev and John Cena had several run-ins leading up to *WrestleMania 31*, where the Bulgarian held his title. Rusev rode into the ring on a massive tank to intimidate Cena.

SUPER STATS

HEIGHT: 6ft (1.82m)

WEIGHT: 304lbs (137.89kg)

HOMETOWN: Plovdiv, Bulgaria

SIGNATURE MOVE: The Accolade—Rusev sits on his opponent's back, and pulls their shoulders back to submission.

MAIN RIVALS: John Cena, Sheamus

SAMI ZAYN

"NEVER QUIT, NEVER SUBMIT."

That's the attitude that drives Sami Zayn to the top. Passionate about in-ring competition and ever the underdog, Zayn puts everything he has into his matches. He's never willing to submit or run away from a challenge. A former NXT Champion, Zayn is determined to fight, scratch, and climb his way to back to championship success.

Trademark cap

ZAYN OVER BRAUN

Braun Strowman demanded "better competition" on *RAW*. Zayn stepped up to the challenge, battling Strowman with his full arsenal of moves, including a high-flying Moonsault.

SUPER STATS

HEIGHT: 6ft 1in (1.85m)

WEIGHT: 212lbs (96kg)

HOMETOWN: Montreal, Quebec, Canada

SIGNATURE MOVE: Helluva Kick —Zayn gives a straight-leg kick to his opponent at the top of their body.

MAIN RIVALS: Braun Strowman, Kevin Owens

SAMOA JOE

A RELENTLESS MERCENARY, "The Destroyer" Samoa Joe enjoys crushing opponents in the ring. He punishes his adversaries with his mixed martial arts-inspired battle style. Joe was the first two-time NXT Champion and he won the first Dusty Rhodes Tag Team tournament with Finn Bálor. Samoa Joe has the WWE Universal Championship in his sights, and will destroy anyone who stands in his way.

Fists of fury, ready for total destruction

DESTROY!

Triple H brought Joe from NXT to *RAW* to be his personal "Destroyer," taking care of Superstars who Triple H feels are out of line. Triple H's first target was Seth Rollins, who Samoa Joe attacked on command.

Loose shorts for mixed martial arts style

SUPER STATS

HEIGHT: 6ft 2in (1.87m)

WEIGHT: 282lbs (127.91kg)

HOMETOWN: Huntington Beach, California

SIGNATURE MOVE: Coquina Clutch—Samoa Joe jams his arm around his opponent's neck from behind.

MAIN RIVALS: Seth Rollins, Brock Lesnar

SASHA BANKS

SHE CALLS HERSELF "The Boss," and with good reason—she's become a multi-time WWE Women's Champion. Starting out in NXT, scrappy Superstar Banks proved her incredible talent would take her to the top. From there, she joined WWE, dominating *RAW*. You know, like a boss!

Brass knuckle rings

HELL IN A CELL

Banks's and Charlotte Flair's rivalry over the *RAW* Women's Championship was incredibly heated. The pair battled in the first-ever women's Hell in a Cell Match in 2016, with Flair storming to victory.

SUPER STATS

HEIGHT: 5ft 5in (1.65m)

HOMETOWN: Boston, Massachusetts

SIGNATURE MOVE: Bank Statement—Banks pulls back on the upper body of her opponent, causing a submission.

MAIN RIVALS: Charlotte Flair, Bayley

169

SCOTT HALL

DID YOU KNOW?

Hall is a member of The Kliq, a group of WWE Superstars that includes Shawn Michaels, Triple H, Kevin Nash, and X-Pac.

HE CHANGED HISTORY

when he surprised the crowd at *WCW Monday Nitro*. Scott Hall had been a WWE Superstar before that night, and so viewers thought WWE was invading WCW. Hall had in fact gone to WCW to create The New World Order faction that ultimately destroyed WCW. Hall and the nWo returned to WWE in 2002, where Hall battled Stone Cold Steve Austin at *WrestleMania X8*.

Chewed on a toothpick as Razor Ramon

Original version of the nWo t-shirt and logo

RAZOR RAMON

Hall competed in WWE under the name Razor Ramon. As four-time Intercontinental Champion, Ramon oozed machismo. Hall joined the WWE Hall of Fame in 2014 in Ramon's name.

SUPER STATS

HEIGHT: 6ft 7in (2.01m)

WEIGHT: 287lbs (130.18kg)

HOMETOWN: Miami, Florida

SIGNATURE MOVE: Razor's Edge —Hall lifts his opponent high above his head by their shoulders and throws them down to the mat.

MAIN RIVALS: Shawn Michaels, Stone Cold Steve Austin

SETH ROLLINS

Shield design is a callback to his leadership in the faction of the same name

A BRILLIANT TACTICIAN,
Seth Rollins takes stock and then decides what to do to win, which has earned him the nickname "The Architect." He recruited Dean Ambrose and Roman Reigns to form The Shield faction. When he no longer needed them, he attacked his teammates. The first-ever NXT Champion, Rollins has also won the WWE Tag Team, United States, and World Championships.

DID YOU KNOW?
Rollins won an eight-man battle called the Gold Rush Tournament to become the first NXT Champion.

Ring gear represents a knight's armor

CASHING IN
Rollins won the 2014 Money in the Bank briefcase, earning a contract for a WWE Championship Match. He "cashed in" the briefcase at *WrestleMania 31* during the battle between Brock Lesnar and Roman Reigns and managed to steal the Title.

SUPER STATS

HEIGHT: 6ft 1in (1.85m)

WEIGHT: 217lbs (98.40kg)

HOMETOWN: Davenport, Iowa

SIGNATURE MOVE: Pedigree—Rollins holds his opponent face down under their shoulders, jumps, and slams them down.

MAIN RIVALS: Triple H, Roman Reigns

SGT. SLAUGHTER

ATTENTION, MAGGOTS! Sgt. Slaughter is here to lead the WWE Universe into combat. A former US Marine Corps drill sergeant, Slaughter brought a brutal level of aggression to the ring. With a deep love for the United States, Slaughter patriotically defended his country. He battled continually with his rival, The Iron Sheik, who liked to bombard him with insults. Slaughter retired in 1997 and became Commissioner of WWE.

Drill sergeant's hat

Camo suit reflects military background

FRIEND OR FOE?

For a brief time during the 1990s, Sgt. Slaughter turned his back on the United States, claiming it was going soft. He apparently allied himself with the nation of Iraq and expressed his contempt of WWE.

SUPER STATS

HEIGHT: 6ft 4in (1.93m)

WEIGHT: 310lbs (140.61kg)

HOMETOWN: Parris Island, South Carolina

SIGNATURE MOVE: Cobra Clutch —Sarge sits on his opponent's back, and pulls their shoulders back

MAIN RIVALS: The Iron Sheik, Pat Patterson

SHANE MCMAHON

BEING THE SON of the WWE Chairman, Vince McMahon, can be a challenge, but Shane McMahon has overcome that challenge and stepped out of his father's shadow. He once purchased WWE's competition, WCW, and tried to take over his father's company. A former WWE European and Hardcore Champion, McMahon left WWE in 2009, but returned in 2016 to lead *SmackDown Live*.

New custom jersey made for each match

MEGAMOVES

McMahon has been known to go to extreme and risky lengths to win matches. He'll dive off incredibly high structures, including the Cell at *WrestleMania 32*, to try to defeat his opponents.

SUPER STATS

HEIGHT: 6ft 2in (1.87m)

WEIGHT: 230lbs (104.32kg)

HOMETOWN: New York City, New York

SIGNATURE MOVE: Coast-to-Coast —Shane McMahon seats his opponent in the ring corner, and jumps from the opposite corner with a fierce kick.

MAIN RIVALS: Kurt Angle, AJ Styles

SHAWN MICHAELS

NO ONE COULD HAVE imagined, when Shawn Michaels began his WWE career as a baby-faced high-flying member of the tag team the Rockers, that he'd become the most celebrated Superstar of all time. Cocky, defiant, and supremely talented, "The Heartbreak Kid" had more classic matches and made more memorable moments than any other Superstar. WWE was Michaels life and passion. A founder of D-Generation X, Michaels was inducted into the WWE Hall of Fame in 2011.

Tattoo symbolizes Michaels' nickname— The Heartbreak Kid

Fists balled and ready for action

LIVE THE DREAM

Michaels's childhood dream was to win the WWE Championship, and his dream came true at *WrestleMania XII*, where he bested Bret "Hit Man" Hart in a 60-minute Iron Man Match.

SUPER STATS

HEIGHT: 6ft 1in (1.85m)

WEIGHT: 225lbs (102kg)

HOMETOWN: San Antonio, Texas

SIGNATURE MOVE: Sweet Chin Music—Michaels kicks his opponent in the chin.

MAIN RIVALS: Undertaker, Bret "Hit Man" Hart

SHEAMUS

LIKE HIS IRISH ANCESTORS, "The Celtic Warrior" Sheamus fights with a fierceness rarely matched. His awesome strength and fiery temper have pushed him to achieve several world championship reigns. In 2010, Sheamus took the crown in the King of the Ring tournament, then triumphed in the 2012 Royal Rumble Match.

Mohawk resembles flames

CESARO

Sheamus and Cesaro didn't like each other at first. But in a series of seven matches, they earned so much respect for each other they formed a tag team and quickly won the RAW Tag Team Championship.

SUPER STATS

HEIGHT: 6ft 4in (1.93m)

WEIGHT: 267lbs (121.10kg)

HOMETOWN: Dublin, Ireland

SIGNATURE MOVE: Brogue Kick—Sheamus hops on one foot, kicking his opponent with the other.

MAIN RIVALS: Cesaro, Daniel Bryan

SHELTON BENJAMIN

WHEN IT COMES TO athletic ability, few compare to Shelton Benjamin. This versatile Superstar was once nicknamed "The Gold Standard" for his thrilling physical feats. From scaling ladders to performing impossible flips in mid-air, Benjamin redefines human limitations. After a short break from WWE, Benjamin returned in 2017 to team up with Chad Gable and is keen to prove he can't be stopped!

DID YOU KNOW?

Benjamin once held the United States Championship for an impressive 243 days from 2008 to 2009.

GOLD MEDAL MENTOR

Kurt Angle first brought Benjamin to WWE as part of "Team Angle." Under Angle's guidance, Benjamin and his partner Charlie Haas excelled and boldly renamed themselves The World's Greatest Tag Team. The duo captured two WWE Tag Team Championships.

SUPER STATS

HEIGHT: 6ft 2in (1.87m)

WEIGHT: 248lbs (112.49kg)

HOMETOWN: Orangeburg, South Carolina

SIGNATURE MOVE: Paydirt—Shelton leaps and grasps the back of his opponent's head. With his body parallel to the mat, he pulls his opponent down, slamming them chest first.

MAIN RIVALS: Chris Jericho, Carlito

SHINSUKE NAKAMURA

IN JAPAN, Shinsuke Nakamura mastered a type of in-ring competition called "Strong Style," which uses hard-hitting strikes and stinging kicks. He brought this style to WWE when he joined NXT in 2016. Quickly winning the NXT Championship, Nakamura impressed the WWE Universe with his charisma and talent. He left NXT for *SmackDown Live* following *WrestleMania 33* in April 2017, determined to use Strong Style to win the WWE Championship.

Studded jacket adds to tough image

STRONG STYLE

Nakamura faced Samoa Joe for the NXT Championship on several occasions. They traded the Title back and forth, but Nakamura was the ultimate victor thanks to his flying kick during their battle for the Title in 2016.

SUPER STATS

HEIGHT: 6ft 2in (1.87m)

WEIGHT: 229lbs (103.87kg)

HOMETOWN: Kyoto, Japan

SIGNATURE MOVE: Kinshasa Knee Strike—Shinsuke Nakamura runs off the ropes and hits his opponent with his knee.

MAIN RIVALS: Dolph Ziggler, Samoa Joe

SID

UNSTABLE AND DANGEROUS, the Superstar known simply as Sid was a dominant force. He first joined WWE in 1991, calling himself "Sid Justice" and wanting to enforce law and order in WWE. Later, known as "Sycho Sid," he became Shawn Michaels's bodyguard before he attacked Michaels and pursued the WWE Championship for himself. Sid used his great strength and power to capture the WWE and WCW Championships.

SLAMMING SLATER

Sid was one of several legends Heath Slater mocked and insulted as *RAW* approached its 1000th episode in 2012. Sid had no patience for such insults, so he hit Slater with his signature Powerbomb move!

SUPER STATS

HEIGHT: 6ft 9in (2.05m)

WEIGHT: 317lbs (143.78kg)

HOMETOWN: West Memphis, Arkansas

SIGNATURE MOVE: Powerbomb —Sid lifts his opponent to shoulder height and drops them to the mat.

MAIN RIVALS: Undertaker, Shawn Michaels

SIN CARA

Sin Cara has masks in dozens of color combinations

DID YOU KNOW?

"Sin Cara" means "man with no face" in Spanish, which suits the Superstar's mysterious nature.

A HIGH-FLYING SUPERSTAR,
Sin Cara began competing in Lucha Libre, Mexico's version of sports entertainment, aged 15. Sin Cara wears a colorful mask when he competes. He uses amazing aerial maneuvers, soaring above the ring, and landing with a big impact on his opponents. He is a former NXT tag team champion with fellow masked Superstar, Kalisto.

Jacket depicts Sin Cara's electricity in the ring

DOUBLE VISION

A mysterious imposter also claiming to be Sin Cara debuted in late 2011. The original Superstar had to prove he was the true Sin Cara by winning a Mask vs. Mask Match on *SmackDown*.

SUPER STATS

HEIGHT: 5ft 7in (1.70m)

WEIGHT: 198lbs (89.81kg)

HOMETOWN: Mexico City, Mexico

SIGNATURE MOVE: Dragon Bomb —Sin Cara dives off the top rope, flipping in mid-air and lands with his shoulders on his opponent.

MAIN RIVALS: The Ascension, Titus O'Neil

THE SINGH BROTHERS

ALTHOUGH THEY CAME to WWE as individual entrants in the WWE Cruiserweight Classic tournament, The Singh Brothers joined forces and entered the tag team rankings on *SmackDown Live*. But where they have had the greatest impact is in supporting their ally, Superstar Jinder Mahal. They attack his opponents and protect Mahal. The brothers are very loyal to Mahal and to each other.

Dress shirts display their wealth

TRIPLE TROUBLE

When Jinder Mahal was pursuing the WWE Championship held by Randy Orton, the Singh Brothers played a major role in helping Mahal overcome Orton on *SmackDown Live*. They held the champion while Mahal attacked him!

SUPER STATS

NAMES: Samir Singh, Sunil Singh

COMBINED WEIGHT: 273lbs (123.83kg)

SIGNATURE MOVE: Double Superkick—The Singh Brothers hit their opponent with a big kick.

MAIN RIVALS: Randy Orton, The Authors of Pain

STEPHANIE MCMAHON

THIS MCMAHON IS considered WWE royalty. Growing up, her father's pioneering ways inspired her to share his passion for sports entertainment. Stephanie is known as "The Queen of WWE," and she rules over WWE with an iron fist in her role as Commissioner of *RAW*. She demonstrates her ruthlessness by forcing other Superstars into difficult matches and ensuring that she and her family always comes out on top.

DID YOU KNOW?

Stephanie McMahon is a former Women's Champion, having won the Title in 2000.

Mask to show Stephanie is an evil queen

THE AUTHORITY

Stephanie McMahon and her husband, Chief Operating Officer Triple H, are together known as "The Authority." They work as partners in the business and in the ring. Stephanie regularly enters with her husband, including at *WrestleMania 32*.

SUPER STATS

HEIGHT: 5ft 9in (1.75m)

HOMETOWN: Greenwich, Connecticut

KEY MOMENT In 2016, Stephanie was introduced as the Comissioner of *RAW* putting her in competition with her brother Shane who became *SmackDown* Commissioner.

MAIN RIVALS: Shane McMahon, Brie Bella

STING

Baseball bat used to intimidate opponents

A TRUE ICON in WCW, Sting only joined WWE in 2014, toward the end of his 30-year career in sports entertainment. The dark, brooding Superstar believed he was an avenging spirit, protecting WCW from the invasion of Triple H's oppressive nWo faction. He faced Triple H in his first WWE match at *WrestleMania 31*, hoping to put an end to Triple H's abuses of power. "The Stinger" was inducted into the WWE Hall of Fame in 2016.

Scorpions, Sting's symbol, adorn his gloves

A NEW STYLE

Sting won the first of seven World Heavyweight Championships at WCW's *Great American Bash* in 1990. In that era, Sting wore bright colors and had blond hair. His American flag-themed jacket and facepaint were a perfect fit for the event.

SUPER STATS

HEIGHT: 6ft 2in (1.87m)

WEIGHT: 250lbs (113.39kg)

HOMETOWN: Venice Beach, California

SIGNATURE MOVE: Scorpion Death Lock—Sting wraps his legs around his opponent's legs, and pulls them back toward their back in a painful submission move.

MAIN RIVALS: Triple H, Ric Flair

STONE COLD STEVE AUSTIN

ANGRY, FOUL-MOUTHED, and always ready for a fight, Stone Cold Steve Austin is arguably the toughest Superstar to ever set foot in the ring. A powerful brawler, Austin punches and stomps all over his opponents. Austin resists authority—and this rebellious nature has earned him the unwavering support of the WWE Universe, as well as 19 championships and induction into the Hall of Fame.

Austin's signature skull logo

RULE BREAKER

Stone Cold Steve Austin was told to follow the rules and conform to what his boss, Mr. McMahon, expected. Austin was not willing to comply; he intentionally broke the rules and gave Mr. McMahon a "Stone Cold Stunner" every chance he got.

SUPER STATS

HEIGHT: 6ft 2in (1.87m)

WEIGHT: 252lbs (114.30kg)

HOMETOWN: Victoria, Texas

SIGNATURE MOVE: Stone Cold Stunner—Austin holds his opponent over his shoulder and drops to the mat, bouncing them backward.

MAIN RIVALS: The Rock, Bret "Hit Man" Hart

SUPERSTAR BILLY GRAHAM

AHEAD OF HIS TIME, boastful Superstar Billy Graham wore tie-dye outfits and feather boas in an era when his fellow competitors dressed more conservatively and tried to let their in-ring actions do all the talking. But Graham could back up his boasts. He won the WWE Championship in 1977 and was inducted into the WWE Hall of Fame in 2004.

DID YOU KNOW?

Billy Graham was trained by WWE Hall of Famer, Stu Hart.

Colorful style was considered too showy by some Superstars and managers

KING DETHRONED

Superstar Billy Graham captured the WWE Championship from Bruno Sammartino in 1977, ending Sammartino's record-holding 4,040-day run as champion.

SUPER STATS

HEIGHT: 6ft 4in (1.93m)

WEIGHT: 275lbs (124.73kg)

HOMETOWN: Paradise Valley, Arizona

SIGNATURE MOVE: Bear Hug —Graham holds his opponent tightly around the waist.

MAIN RIVALS: Bruno Sammartino, Bob Backlund

TAMINA

Fierce expression demonstrates Tamina's ambitious attitude

DEBUTING WITH HER cousins The Usos in 2011, Tamina is a Superstar with a chip on her shoulder. She is out to prove that she is the most dominant female in WWE. It's working—she uses her power and high-flying arsenal to intimidate those in *SmackDown Live*'s women's division. Tamina has been a bodyguard and a manager, and now hopes to become SmackDown Women's Champion.

TEAM B.A.D.

In 2015, WWE's Women's Revolution added several female competitors to the WWE roster. Tamina joined forces with Sasha Banks and Naomi to form a stable named Team B.A.D. (Beautiful And Dangerous) that aimed to help members of the group rise through the ranks of the women's divison.

SUPER STATS

HEIGHT: 5ft 9in (1.75m)

HOMETOWN: The Pacific Islands

SIGNATURE MOVE: Superfly Splash—Tamina dives off the top rope, landing hard on her opponent.

MAIN RIVALS: Naomi, Nikki Bella

TATANKA

Special headdress worn in honor of Tatanka's people and culture

HIS WAR CRY sounding throughout the arena, Tatanka proudly represented his people— the Lumbee Native American Tribe— as a fierce Superstar. He prepared for every match by performing a Lumbee war dance, and was presented with a sacred chief's headdress on *RAW* in recognition of his in-ring accomplishments.

Tomahawk is a traditional Native American tool and weapon

FLYING HIGH

Tatanka used his range of great fighting skills, including flying dives from the top of the ring, to remain undefeated until December 1993—after nearly two years as an unbeaten competitor.

SUPER STATS

HEIGHT: 6ft 2in (1.87m)

WEIGHT: 285lbs (129kg)

HOMETOWN: Pembroke, North Carolina

SIGNATURE MOVE: Indian Death Drop—Tatanka holds his opponent on his shoulders and drops backward to the mat.

MAIN RIVALS: Lex Luger, IRS

TERRY FUNK

THE ORIGINAL HARDCORE

competitor, Terry Funk spent 50 years competing in Hardcore Matches, where weapons were common and the danger was real. Funk was a second-generation Superstar, learning his skills from his father, Dory Funk. He fought in matches all over the world and was a former World Heavyweight Champion. Funk competed in WWE under a mask, with the name "Chainsaw Charlie." He was inducted to the WWE Hall of Fame in 2009.

Logo represents Funk's sports entertainment training school, Funk U

ECW CHAMPION

More than 25 years after winning his first World Heavyweight Championship in 1970, Terry Funk won the ECW Championship at the first-ever ECW pay-per-view event, *Barely Legal*, in 1997.

SUPER STATS

HEIGHT: 6ft 1in (1.85m)

WEIGHT: 246lbs (111.58kg)

HOMETOWN: Amarillo, Texas

SIGNATURE MOVE: Spinning Toe Hold—Funk twists his opponent's leg around his own and applies pressure to their foot.

MAIN RIVALS: Ric Flair, Mick Foley

TITUS O'NEIL

NO ONE IN WWE

lives life with as much drive and passion as Titus O'Neil. O'Neil burst into WWE in 2012 as one half of the Prime Time Players tag team with Darren Young. After they won the Tag Team Championship in 2015, O'Neil chose to leave Young and pursue singles competition. O'Neil believes his self-perception of his talent in the ring will lead him to championship glory.

DID YOU KNOW?

O'Neil, a former Florida Gators college football player, once formed a tag team with Heath Slater called Slater Gator.

A sharp suit represents O'Neil's quest for excellence

TITUS WORLDWIDE

Titus O'Neil runs a stable of Superstars called Titus Worldwide. The participants need to live up to O'Neil's level of excellence. So far, the stable has included Apollo Crews, Akira Tozawa, and even celebrity rapper Wale.

SUPER STATS

HEIGHT: 6ft 6in (1.98m)

WEIGHT: 270lbs (122.47kg)

HOMETOWN: Live Oak, Florida

SIGNATURE MOVE: Clash of the Titus—O'Neil lifts his opponent high above his head and slams them to the mat.

MAIN RIVALS: The New Day, Big Show

TJP

LIKE A LIVING VIDEO-GAME character, TJP performs incredible tricks and moves in the ring. A high flyer with a large ego, TJP joined WWE representing the Phillipines in the WWE Cruiserweight Classic. The former Cruiserweight Champion is a foundational part of WWE's cruiserweight division on *RAW* and *205 Live*. TJP is certain he will be champion again, flying past all other Superstars.

Jacket looks like it could be worn by a video-game character

A NEW CHAMPION

In 2016, WWE invited Superstars who weighed 205 pounds (92.98kg) or less to compete in the Cruiserweight Classic tournament. TJP defeated Gran Metalik in the final to win the tournament and be crowned the very first Cruiserweight Champion.

Sun symbol represents the flag of the Philippines

SUPER STATS

HEIGHT: 5ft 10in (1.77m)

WEIGHT: 167lbs (75.74kg)

HOMETOWN: Los Angeles, California

SIGNATURE MOVE: Kneebar— TJP wraps his legs and arm around his opponent's leg and knee and applies pressure on their kneecap.

MAIN RIVALS: The Brian Kendrick, Neville

TOMMASO CIAMPA

FORMERLY ONE-HALF of the tag team #DIY alongside his ex-best friend Johnny Gargano, Tommaso Ciampa attacked his partner at *NXT Takeover: Chicago* and declared himself the most dangerous man in sports entertainment. With a vicious streak and impressive technical skills in the ring, Ciampa is sure to achieve greatness in WWE. But his friends had better beware—he'll betray anyone to get what he wants.

Eyes betray Ciampa's devious mind

A FRIENDSHIP ENDS

After losing their match to reclaim the NXT Tag Team Championship at *NXT TakeOver: Chicago 2017*, Tommaso Ciampa attacked Johnny Gargano, ending the tag team and a lifelong friendship.

SUPER STATS

HEIGHT: 5ft 11in (1.80m)

WEIGHT: 201lbs (91.17kg)

HOMETOWN: Milwaukee, Wisconsin

SIGNATURE MOVE: Armbar— Ciampa holds tight to his opponent's arm, applying pressure to the elbow and shoulder.

MAIN RIVALS: Johnny Gargano, The Revival

TONY NESE

IT TAKES A LOT of confidence to call oneself "The Premier Athlete," but Tony Nese has that much confidence—and more. He joined WWE as a participant in the Cruiserweight Classic tournament in 2016. He uses his impressive physique and a variety of skills and moves to win his matches. Neither exclusively an aerial flyer nor a mat technician, it's his combination of styles that have brought Nese success in the cruiserweight division.

Gauntlet-style wrist wraps protect wrists during matches

Nese claims to have an "eight pack" of abdominal muscles rather than the usual six

THE INDEPENDENTS

Tony Nese, like many current Superstars, such as Daniel Bryan and Seth Rollins, refined his in-ring skills in smaller, non-WWE sports entertainment companies around the world called "Independents." Nese was one of several Independent Superstars invited by WWE to participate in the 2016 Cruiserweight Classic tournament where he competed against the likes of The Brian Kendrick.

SUPER STATS

HEIGHT: 5ft 9in (1.75m)

WEIGHT: 196lbs (88.9kg)

HOMETOWN: Long Island, New York

SIGNATURE MOVE: 450 Splash —Nese dives off the top rope and turns 45 degrees in the air before landing on his opponent.

MAIN RIVALS: TJP, Rich Swann

TRIPLE H

Triple H studies his opponents' techniques extensively before matches

FOR MORE THAN two decades, Triple H has been one of the most dominant Superstars in WWE. The 14-time World Champion goes by many nicknames, including "The Game" and "The King of Kings." He is a strategic genius in the ring, knowing exactly how to attack his opponents physically and mentally. Outside the ring, in his role as WWE's Chief Operating Officer, Triple H controls matches and shapes the destinies of the WWE Superstars.

WORLD CHAMPION

Triple H won his 14th World Championship at the 2016 Royal Rumble Match. He defeated 29 other Superstars to capture the Title.

SUPER STATS

HEIGHT: 6ft 4in (1.93m)

WEIGHT: 255lbs (115.66kg)

HOMETOWN: Greenwich, Connecticut

SIGNATURE MOVE: Pedigree —Triple H hooks his bent-over opponent by his arms and jumps up, slamming them to the ground.

MAIN RIVALS: Undertaker, Seth Rollins

TRISH STRATUS

BEGINNING HER CAREER as a manager, Trish Stratus fell in love with in-ring competition and made it her goal to become the best female Superstar in WWE history. As a seven-time WWE Women's Champion, she's certainly a contender. With tremendous athletic ability, Stratus redefined expectations of women in the ring and built the foundations for female sports entertainment, which today is stronger than ever. Stratus was inducted into the WWE Hall of Fame in 2013.

Strength assisted by a mastery of yoga

MAIN STARS

In 2004, Trish Stratus and Lita entered the WWE record books by being the first women to compete in a main event on *RAW*.

SUPER STATS

HEIGHT: 5ft 5in (1.65m)

HOMETOWN: Toronto, Ontario, Canada

SIGNATURE MOVE: Stratusfaction—Trish holds the top of her opponent's body, runs up the ropes and bounces off them, dragging them to the mat.

MAIN RIVALS: Lita, Mickie James

TYE DILLINGER

ON A SCALE of one to ten, Tye Dillinger always gives himself a "Perfect 10." He believes wholeheartedly that his good looks and abilities in the ring are the very best in the world. He will even grade his performance mid-match, pausing to hold up his ten fingers or share a fan's ringside scorecard. After competing in NXT from 2013 to 2017, Dillinger joined *SmackDown Live* to show a new group of admirers what a "Perfect 10" really looks like.

Dazzling jacket is a perfect look, in Dillinger's opinion

Favorite number emblazoned on ring gear

PERFECT 10

Dillinger made his WWE pay-per-view debut in the 2017 Royal Rumble Match. He didn't win the battle, but he was pleased to enter the 30-Superstar battle at his favorite spot: number 10.

SUPER STATS

HEIGHT: 6ft 3in (1.90m)

WEIGHT: 223lbs (101.15kg)

HOMETOWN: Niagara Falls, Ontario, Canada

SIGNATURE MOVE: Tye Breaker —Dillinger holds his opponent on his shoulders and flips them down, crashing them on his knee before they hit the mat.

MAIN RIVALS: Bobby Roode, Eric Young

ULTIMATE WARRIOR

Face painted in with different designs for every match

WITH FRENETIC ENERGY, Ultimate Warrior would run to the ring, violently shake the ropes, and electrify the WWE Universe. The former WWE Champion was known for his fast-paced, hard-hitting in-ring style. The face-painted Superstar captivated the imaginations of a generation, teaching his "little Warriors" to believe in the power of dreams. He achieved his greatest dream when he was inducted into the WWE Hall of Fame in 2014.

Neon arm tassels add to his colorful look

WARRIOR AWARD

Every year at the WWE Hall of Fame Ceremony, in memory of the Ultimate Warrior, a special Warrior Award is presented to an individual who has overcome difficult challenges in their life.

SUPER STATS

HEIGHT: 6ft 2in (1.87m)

WEIGHT: 280lbs (127kg)

HOMETOWN: Parts Unknown

SIGNATURE MOVE: Gorilla Press Slam—Ultimate Warrior holds his opponent high above his head and drops them behind him.

MAIN RIVALS: "Macho Man" Randy Savage, Undertaker

UMAGA

DID YOU KNOW?

Umaga was WWE Hall of Famer Rikishi's brother, and an uncle to the Usos.

Face painted in traditional Samoan war paint

WITH AN APPETITE for destruction, Umaga, "The Samoan Bulldozer," devastated opponents and wreaked havoc throughout WWE. He defeated Jeff Hardy to become the Intercontinental Champion in 2007, and served as a bodyguard for the McMahon family. His size and agility made him a dangerous competitor who was feared by the many Superstars he faced in the ring. Umaga has left a lasting legacy in WWE, with many memorable moments in the ring.

Taped thumb makes Umaga's Samoan Spike signature move even more painful

BATTLE OF THE BILLIONAIRES

At *WrestleMania 23*, Umaga (with his manager Armando Estrada ringside) represented Mr. McMahon in the "Battle of the Billionaires," facing off against Bobby Lashley, who represented billionaire Donald Trump.

SUPER STATS

HEIGHT: 6ft 4in (1.93m)

WEIGHT: 350lbs (158.75kg)

HOMETOWN: Samoa

SIGNATURE MOVE: Samoan Spike—Umaga jabs his thumb into the upper part of his opponent's body.

MAIN RIVALS: John Cena, Triple H

UNDERTAKER

FROM THE MOMENT he first walked to the ring at the *1990 Survivor Series*, Undertaker has inspired awe and fear in all those who encounter him. With abilities that seem supernatural, Undertaker laid the biggest names in WWE history to rest in his matches. He is a seven-time WWE Champion, and has helped create unique matches such as Buried Alive and Casket Matches.

Tattoos features the Grim Reaper and other images of destruction

This style of glove is worn by mixed martial arts fighters

WRESTLEMANIA STREAK

For two decades, Undertaker built up the greatest *WrestleMania* winning streak in WWE history. Undertaker won 21 *WrestleMania* matches in a row before his first loss to Brock Lesnar, at *WrestleMania 30*.

SUPER STATS

HEIGHT: 6ft 10in (2.08m)

WEIGHT: 309lbs (140.16kg)

HOMETOWN: Death Valley

SIGNATURE MOVE: Tombstone —Undertaker holds his opponent upside down and drops them to the mat.

MAIN RIVALS: Shawn Michaels, Brock Lesnar

THE USOS

THESE TWIN BROTHERS are unlike any other tag team in WWE. As second-generation Superstars, Jimmy and Jey Uso were trained for in-ring competition by their father, WWE Hall of Famer Rikishi, from a very young age. The identical twins display lots of energy in the ring, working in perfect unison. For years, The Usos were a happy, fun-loving duo, but in 2016 they took on an angrier, more aggressive attitude.

Jimmy's traditional Samoan tattoos pay tribute to The Uso's heritage

TAG CHAMPS

Thanks to their new more aggressive attitudes, The Usos defeated their rivals American Alpha to win the SmackDown Tag Team Championship in 2017.

SUPER STATS

NAMES: Jimmy Uso, Jey Uso

COMBINED WEIGHT: 479lbs (217.27kg)

HOMETOWN: San Francisco, California

SIGNATURE MOVE: Double Samoan Splash—Both Usos dive off the top rope on to their opponent.

MAIN RIVALS: The New Day, American Alpha

VADER

"V" gesture is Vader's favorite pose

WHAT TIME IS IT? It's Vader time! Known as "the Mastadon," Vader was a massive giant who flew through the air like a cruiserweight. A three-time WCW World Heavyweight Champion, Vader came to WWE in 1997 and soon showed off his violent temperament by attacking WWE President, Gorilla Monsoon. After being suspended for that heinous act, Vader battled Goldust and defeated him at the 1998 *Royal Rumble*. Vader retired from full-time in-ring competition later that year.

IT'S VADER TIME FOR STING

Vader's biggest rival for the WCW World Heavyweight Championship was the Superstar Sting. Vader used his mammoth frame to defeat Sting on several occasions, including two tussles for the World Championship.

SUPER STATS

HEIGHT: 6ft 5in (1.95m)

WEIGHT: 450lbs (204.12kg)

HOMETOWN: The Rocky Mountains

SIGNATURE MOVE: Vaderbomb—Vader jumps off the second rope, crashing on top of his opponent.

MAIN RIVALS: Sting, Mick Foley

VISCERA

ONE OF THE LARGEST Superstars to ever compete in a WWE ring, Viscera rose to prominence as a member of Undertaker's Ministry of Darkness stable. Once freed from Undertaker's ministry, Viscera took on the nickname "World's Biggest Love Machine," and began courting the women of WWE and chasing off Superstars he saw as competitive suitors.

Eyes turned white when he joined the Ministry of Darkness

Comfortable robe for battling in the ring

KING MABEL

Viscera was named "Mabel" while part of the Men on a Mission tag team. After splitting from the team and winning the 1995 *King of the Ring* tournament, the Superstar declared himself "King Mabel" and wore a crown at all times.

SUPER STATS

HEIGHT: 6ft 9in (2.05m)

WEIGHT: 487lbs (221kg)

HOMETOWN: Harlem, New York

SIGNATURE MOVE: Viscera Driver —Viscera lifts his opponent into the air with both hands and throws them down to the mat.

MAIN RIVALS: Undertaker, Mark Henry

WARLORD

DID YOU KNOW?
The Warlord and his partners defeated Dusty Rhodes and partners to win the WCW Six-Man Tag Team Championship in 1988.

BUILDING HIS CAREER as one half of a tag team known as "The Powers of Pain," The Warlord was among the strongest competitors in WWE in the 1990s. The Warlord destroyed his adversaries in both the tag team and singles divisions with his unbreakable Full Nelson submission hold. His size and aggression made him a seemingly unstoppable force throughout his career.

Wand used to punish opponents

BATTLING THE BULLDOG

The Warlord's highest profile match was at *WrestleMania VII* against "The British Bulldog" Davey Boy Smith. Though The Warlord came up short in the match, it was an even battle between the two that either Superstar could have won.

SUPER STATS

HEIGHT: 6ft 5in (1.95m)

WEIGHT: 323lbs (146.51kg)

HOMETOWN: Parts Unknown

SIGNATURE MOVE: Full Nelson— The Warlord holds his hands behind his opponent's shoulders and lifts their arms up in a painful submission hold.

MAIN RIVALS: British Bulldog, Bushwhackers

WENDI RICHTER

IN THE 1980S, before WWE's Women's Revolution, even before there were "Divas," there was Wendi Richter. A two-time Women's Champion, Richter helped grow WWE into a worldwide phenomenon. Richter's fiercely fought matches were dynamic and exciting. Matches against her greatest rival, Lelani Kai, were especially popular, including when they battled each other at the first *WrestleMania* in 1985. Richter was inducted into the WWE Hall of Fame in 2010.

Typical 1980s hairstyle

Richter's outfit was standard for a female Superstar in 1980s WWE

FAMOUS FRIENDS

On the road to *WrestleMania I*, Wendi Richter needed help fending off the attacks from her enemy, Lelani Kai. She found that help in rock star Cyndi Lauper, who also helped Richter train.

SUPER STATS

HEIGHT: 5ft 8in (1.72m)

HOMETOWN: Dallas, Texas

SIGNATURE MOVE: Sitout DDT—Richter grabs her opponent and pulls them down to the mat shoulders first.

MAIN RIVAL: Fabulous Moolah, Lelani Kai

WESLEY BLAKE AND STEVE CUTLER

Matching jackets show tag team unity

AFTER A SURPRISING split from his longtime tag team partner Buddy Murphy, with whom he won the NXT Tag Team Championship in 2015, Wesley Blake ventured out on his own seeking singles stardom. Along the way he met Steve Cutler, an inexperienced NXT rookie, and took the rising Superstar under his wing. Together Blake and Cutler are forging a strong bond as a tag team, and fighting their way through the NXT tag team division, on a quest to capture the championship.

TEXAS ROOTS

Wesley Blake was mentored by Dory Funk Jr, a WWE Hall of Famer who rose to fame in the gritty Amarillo, Texas wrestling scene. When he first arrived at NXT, Blake paid homage to Funk and his home state by wearing a cowboy hat and living by the motto "Cowboy Up."

SUPER STATS

NAMES: Steve Cutler, Wesley Blake

COMBINED WEIGHT: 465lbs (210.92kg)

SIGNATURE MOVE: Frog Splash—Blake dives off the top rope, landing on his opponent with a hard thud.

MAIN RIVAL: Heavy Machinery

WILD SAMOANS

JUST AS THEIR NAME implies, the Wild Samoans were unpredictable in the ring. Opponents were terrified of facing the brothers because they never knew what the Wild Samoans would do to secure a win. Together, Afa and Sika won three Tag Team Championships. Following their retirement in 1988, the Wild Samoans served as trainers and managers for new Superstars. They were inducted into the WWE Hall of Fame in 2007.

"Lavalava," traditional Samoan clothing

ROCKY ROAD

Among the Wild Samoans' greatest rivals for Championships was Rocky Johnson. The Wild Samoans had countless matches against the Superstar, including their defeat of him for the Tag Team Championship.

SUPER STATS

NAMES: Sika, Afa

COMBINED WEIGHT: 645lbs (292.56kg)

HOMETOWN: Samoa

SIGNATURE MOVE: Samoan Drop—The Wild Samoans hold an opponent on their shoulders and drop back, slamming them down.

MAIN RIVALS: Bob Backlund, Rocky Johnson

X-PAC

AFTER A SHOCKING win over Superstar Razor Ramon on a 1993 episode of *Monday Night RAW*, X-Pac, then known as the 1-2-3 Kid, began a journey that would make him one of the most recognized Superstars in WWE history. X-Pac was rebellious and joined nWo and D-Generation X factions hoping to cause chaos in WWE. But he was also successful in the ring. He held the WWE Tag Team, European, Light Heavyweight, United States, and Cruiserweight championships during his amazing 20-year career.

Green and black are the colors of D-Generation X

BACK WITH DX

X-Pac achieved his greatest success while he was a member of the D-Generation X faction. He reunited with members Shawn Michaels, Triple H, and The New Age Outlaws on the 1000th episode of *RAW* in 2012.

SUPER STATS

HEIGHT: 6ft 1in (1.85m)

WEIGHT: 212lbs (96kg)

HOMETOWN: Minneapolis, Minnesota

SIGNATURE MOVE: X-Factor— X-Pac grabs his opponents by their hair and drags them to the mat.

MAIN RIVALS: Chris Jericho, Ric Flair

YOKOZUNA

Long hair held in a tight bun

THE EPITOME OF a "super heavyweight," Yokozuna joined WWE in 1992 following his success competing in sumo wrestling in Japan. Upon his arrival, Yokozuna used his insurmountable weight advantage to win the 1993 Royal Rumble Match, which earned him a WWE Championship Match at *WrestleMania IX*. He won his first of two WWE Championships at *WrestleMania IX*, defeating Bret "Hit Man" Hart. Yokozuna joined the WWE Hall of Fame in 2012.

MR. FUJI

Throughout his entire career, Yokozuna was accompanied to the ring by his manager, Mr. Fuji. Fuji was devious and liked to help his charges win by cheating whenever necessary. Fuji was inducted into the WWE Hall of Fame in 2007.

The tassels on a high-ranking sumo wrestler's belt (or mawashi) represent status as a competitor.

SUPER STATS

HEIGHT: 6ft 4in (1.93m)

WEIGHT: 589lbs (267.16kg)

HOMETOWN: The Land of the Rising Sun

SIGNATURE MOVE: Banzai Drop —Yokozuna jumps off the middle rope and lands in a seated position on his opponent.

MAIN RIVALS: Bret "Hit Man" Hart, Undertaker

ZACK RYDER

Dark sunglasses—because Ryder believes his future is so bright

HARNESSING THE POWER of social media to interact with the WWE Universe and build up massive support, Zack Ryder is a Superstar for the modern era. Ryder used his popularity to motivate himself to reach championship glory and he has managed to grab the United States and Intercontinental Championships. Ryder continues to strive for greatness, pumping his fist and shouting his trademark call, "Woo! Woo! Woo!" along with his fans.

Logo features a stylish combination of Ryder's initials

FAME AND GLORY

After defeating six other Superstars, (Kevin Owens, Sami Zayn, Stardust, The Miz, Dolph Ziggler, and Sin Cara) Zack Ryder climbed a ladder and grabbed the Intercontinental Title, winning the Championship and even more glory.

SUPER STATS

HEIGHT: 6ft 2in (1.87m)

WEIGHT: 224lbs (101.6kg)

HOMETOWN: Long Island, New York

SIGNATURE MOVE: Rough Ryder —Ryder jumps high in the air, wraps his legs around his opponent's shoulders, and pulls them to the mat.

MAIN RIVALS: Dolph Ziggler, The Miz

DK | Penguin Random House

Editor Pamela Afram
Senior Designer Lauren Adams
Designers James McKeag, Rhys Thomas,
Thelma Jane Robb
Pre-Production Producer Siu Yin Chan
Producer Lloyd Robertson
Managing Editor Paula Regan
Managing Art Editor Jo Connor
Art Director Lisa Lanzarini
Publisher Julie Ferris
Publishing Director Simon Beecroft

Global Publishing Manager Steve Pantaleo
Vice President, North American Licensing Jess Richardson
Executive Vice President, Consumer Products Casey Collins
Photo department Josh Tottenham, Frank Vitucci,
Georgiana Dallas, Jamie Nelson, Melissa Halladay,
Mike Moran, JD Sestito
Vice President, Intellectual Property Lauren Dienes-Middlen
Senior Vice President, Creative Services Stan Stanski
Creative Director John Jones
Project Manager Sara Vazquez

Dorling Kindersley would also like to thank Laura Buller, Joseph Stewart,
Julia March, and Hannah Gulliver-Jones for editorial assistance.

First American Edition, 2018
Published in the United States by DK Publishing
345 Hudson Street, New York, New York 10014

Page design copyright ©2018 Dorling Kindersley Limited
DK, a Division of Penguin Random House LLC
18 19 20 21 22 10 9 8 7 6 5 4 3 2 1
001–305861–March/2018

A catalog record for this book is available from the Library of Congress.

ISBN 978-1-4654-6783-6

DK books are available at special discounts when purchased in bulk for sales
promotions, premiums, fund-raising, or educational use. For details, contact:
DK Publishing Special Markets, 345 Hudson Street, New York, New York 10014
SpecialSales@dk.com

Photographs on pages 43, 65, 67, 112, 125, 184, and 187
courtesy of *Pro Wrestling Illustrated*.

Printed and bound in China

A WORLD OF IDEAS:
SEE ALL THERE IS TO KNOW
www.wwe.com
www.dk.com